**JANE'S POCKET BOOK
ARMIES OF THE WORLD**

JANE'S POCKET BOOK
ARMIES OF THE WORLD

Compiled by Colonel John Weeks

JANE'S
LONDON   SYDNEY

FIRST PUBLISHED 1981

COPYRIGHT © John Weeks 1981

ISBN 0 7106 0149 2

This edition is not available for sale in the United States, its
dependencies, the Philippine Islands or the Dominion of
Canada

Printed in Great Britain by
Netherwood Dalton and Co. Ltd., Huddersfield

PUBLISHED BY JANE'S PUBLISHING COMPANY LTD
238 CITY ROAD, LONDON EC1V 2PU

INTRODUCTION

There are innumerable books dealing with the armies of the world. They approach the subject from every conceivable direction and in every conceivable amount of detail, examining all aspects or just one or two particular ones, but the great difficulty is to find one volume of a moderate size which gives an overall view and lists the essential factors.

The aim of this Pocket book has been to do that. Within the covers of this small book there is to be found the essential outline details of every army in the world, together with a thumbnail sketch of its history, organisation, structure and an assessment of its capabilities. The main items of equipment are listed by categories and their country of origin noted. This, we believe, is sufficient to give the reader a clear idea of the state of any army and an idea of its military effectiveness. It is a small, handy reference work for the busy person who needs to look up detail quickly and who either does not own, or does not have access to, the full library from which this pocket book has been distilled.

Each country is listed alphabetically and is treated separately. No attempt has been made to introduce the military groupings and treaty obligations that bind one country to another or to several others. We believe that the users of this pocket book are likely to be needing a basis of comparison between two or more armies and with that likely use in mind we have retained the same layout framework for all so that a quick glance is enough to make direct comparisons in each listed special area. Inevitably space has constricted each entry and some use has been made of abbreviations. These are explained in the Glossary.

John Weeks

May 1981

GLOSSARY

AA	Anti-aircraft
AFV	Armoured fighting vehicle. A generic name for all tracked or wheeled armoured military vehicles that carry guns or other offensive equipment
APC	Armoured personnel carrier
ATGW	Anti-tank guided weapon
ATk	Anti-tank
CVR (T)&(W)	Combat vehicle reconnaissance (tracked) and (wheeled). A series of light AFVs designed and built in UK
LAA	Light anti-aircraft. Usually applied to AA guns of a calibre in the range 20 mm to 70 mm.
MG	Machine gun
MMG	Medium machine gun
Para-military	Forces organised and equipped in a way closely akin to that of a regular military force, but not expressly an army. Thus, some police forces have well-armed squads carrying infantry weapons which can be used almost as light infantry. The term is also applied to part-time light forces which are not specifically in the Reserve, ie Workers' Militia
Pdr	Pounder, as in 25 pdr. An obsolete way of expressing the size of an artillery gun by the weight of its shell in pounds. British
PRC	People's Republic of China
RCL	Recoilless. Usually taken to mean a recoilless gun
RL	Rocket launcher. An artillery piece which discharges one or more rockets as a support weapon. Generally used in WP and communist armies
SAM	Surface-to-air missile
SMG	Sub-machinegun
SP	Self-propelled. Applied to artillery guns
SSM	Surface-to-surface missile
WP	Warsaw Pact. White Phosphorus when applied to the filling of a munition

AFGHANISTAN

Strength: Last quoted figure was 100 000 but this is likely to be substantially different now due to the Soviet intervention and the mass desertions which have occurred. Reserves numbered 150 000 at the same time together with a gendarmerie of 30 000 and upwards of 200 000 tribal levies

Military service: Two years for conscripts

Structure: The Afghan Army used to consist of ten infantry divisions and three armoured divisions together with mountain brigades and service troops, all organised and equipped on Soviet lines. These divisions were reportedly under-strength and would be made up with reservists on mobilisation. They were largely deployed along the border with Pakistan, with a reserve force in the central region. Training of the regular officers and NCOs was thorough, but the conscripts may have been less well-instructed and after discharge they were only liable for a further 2 months training during the next 22 years. It can be assumed therefore that any reservists recalled after an interval of more than two years could only be used as riflemen in the infantry.

The position and strength of the Afghan Army is so confused since the Soviet invasion that it is unprofitable to speculate on it, but it can be assumed that it will take some time for it to stabilise after the Soviets leave.

3 armoured divisions
10 infantry divisions
3 mountain infantry brigades

Equipment

AFVs Tanks	T-34	(USSR)		200
	T-54/55	(USSR)		500
			(replacing T-34)	
	PT-76	(USSR)		60
APCs	BMP	(USSR)		40
	BTR-40/	(USSR)		400
	50/60/15z	(USSR)		
Artillery	152 mm	(USSR)	⎫	
	122 mm	(USSR)	⎬ 900	
	100 mm	(USSR)	⎪	
	76 mm	(USSR)	⎭	
	132 mm RL	(USSR)		50
	37 mm AA	(USSR)	⎫	
	57 mm AA	(USSR)	⎬ 350	
	85 mm AA	(USSR)	⎪	
	100 mm AA	(USSR)	⎭	
Anti-tank	Sagger ATGW	(USSR)		
	Snapper ATGW	(USSR)		
Mortars	120 mm	(USSR)		100
Infantry	All small arms of Soviet pattern			

9

ALBANIA

Strength: 33 000 (20 000 + conscripts)
Reserves 70 000
Military service: Two years
Background: Albania has not been involved in any military activities since the Second World War. The state of training and the standard of leadership cannot be assessed, but it is generally assumed that the army would only be capable of limited defence against an invasion and could not sustain any offensive operations for long. A serious liability is the lack of transport and the profusion of different equipment, much of it very old.
Structure: All army formations are below strength and are deployed in two districts inside the country, the north and the south. Their twin tasks are the defence of the state and the maintenance of law and order.

1 tank brigade
6 infantry brigades
8 coast artillery battalions

Equipment

AFVs Tanks	T-34/85	(USSR)	70	
	T-54	(USSR)	30	
	T-62	(USSR)	40	
			(approx)	
APCs	BA-64	(USSR)		
	BTR-60	(USSR)	20	
			(approx)	
	BTR-152	(USSR)		
SP guns	SU-100	(USSR)		
	SU-76	(USSR)		
Artillery	152 mm M43	(USSR)		
	122 mm M38	(USSR)		
	85 mm M45	(USSR)		
	76 mm M42	(USSR)		
	37 mm M38 AA	(USSR)		
	57 mm M50 AA	(USSR)		
	85 mm M44 AA	(USSR)		
Anti-tank	85 mm M45	(USSR)		
	76.2 mm M42	(USSR)		
	57 mm M43,			
	M55	(USSR)		
	45 mm M37	(USSR)		
Mortars	160 mm M43	(USSR)		
	120 mm M43	(USSR)		
	82 mm M37	(USSR)		

Infantry — Infantry weapons are a mixture of Soviet, Chinese and some Second World War German. Almost every Eastern Bloc small arm made since 1945 can be found in use. A peculiarity is that the 14.5 mm PTRD anti-tank rifle is still held on strength.

ALGERIA

Strength: 70 000, all-regular. There is no shortage of volunteers for the forces.
Reserves are estimated to be up to 100 000. There is a separate gendarmerie equipped with infantry weapons
Military service: 6 months. This time is unlikely to be spent in the forces, but in civil works and semi-political education.
Background: The Algerian Army was formed after independence in 1962. The core was taken from the FLN guerrillas who had fought the French and at first the army was a lightly armed, fragmentary force which was soundly beaten in a border conflict with Morocco in 1963. Since then there has been considerable re-organisation and retraining on Soviet lines, though there have been no major wars to try the new army. There is a constant threat of trouble on the southern borders and this, together with the requirement to patrol long land frontiers, keeps most of the army on an active service footing. The threat of a renewed war with Morocco has brought about a steady rise in the arms budget and an improvement in capability which could mean that the Algerian Army is now able to conduct prolonged operations outside its own frontiers.

Structure: The main strength of the army is in the infantry, but despite the comparatively large size there is no apparent attempt to form formations larger than brigade strength and most units act as independent battalions, reflecting the essentially guerrilla and internal security aspect of their employment.

 1 armoured brigade
 4 motorised infantry brigades
 3 independent tank battalions
50 independent infantry battalions
 1 parachute battalion
 7 independent artillery battalions
 7 independent AA battalions
12 companies of specialist desert troops

ALGERIA

Equipment

AFVs Tanks	T-34	(USSR)	100
	AMX-13	(France)	50
	T-54/55/62	(USSR)	350 (approx)
Armoured cars	AML	(France)	30 (approx)
APCs	BTR-40/50/60/152	(USSR)	400 (approx)
SP guns	SU-122/152	(USSR)	15
	SU-100	(USSR)	70
	SU-85	(USSR)	5

Artillery	152 mm M43	(USSR)	
	122 mm M38	(USSR)	600
	85 mm M45	(USSR)	
	240 mm RL	(USSR)	30
	140 mm RL	(USSR)	20
	100 mm AA	(USSR)	
	85 mm AA	(USSR)	
	57 mm AA	(USSR)	
	Frog SSM	(USSR)	15
Mortars	160 mm	(USSR)	80
	120 mm	(USSR)	
Anti-tank	Sagger ATGW	(USSR)	
Infantry	Almost entirely equipped with Soviet weapons		

ANGOLA

Strength: The exact strength is not known, but it has been proposed that it should reach 30 000

Military service: Two years

Background: The independent state of Angola only dates from 1975 and the army has never had the opportunity to stabilise. It is heavily dependent upon aid and direction from Cuba, the Soviet Union and East Germany. It is highly likely that all the mechanised equipment, the artillery and the small numbers of ATGW are in the hands of foreign troops. Internal political feuds and a running border war with Zaïre appear to occupy most of the efforts and time of the Angolan Army.

Structure: It is difficult to be precise about the structure since what is published and what is actually present on the ground may be quite different. It is likely that for the most part the army consists of semi-independent units, loosely grouped into formations for easier administration and communication.

There are said to be
1 tank regiment
1 or more motorised infantry regiments
several infantry regiments
a small number of AA units

Equipment: Almost every variety of Soviet equipment has been seen in Angola since 1975, together with weapons left behind by the Portuguese. There is no indigenous industry so the army is heavily dependent upon its foreign supplies for spares and servicing. An abbreviated list is given below of what has been sighted, but it must not be taken that all of this is necessarily in working order.

AFVs Tanks	T-34	(USSR)	80
	T-54/55	(USSR)	50+
	PT-76	(USSR)	50+
APCs	BTR-40	(USSR)	
	BTR-50	(USSR)	120
	BRDM	(USSR)	
	OT-62	(USSR)	
Artillery	122 mm	(USSR)	
	76 mm	(USSR)	120
	122 mm BM-21 RL	(USSR)	120
	SA-7 SAM	(USSR)	
	Various AA guns		
Mortars	120 mm	(USSR)	300+
	82 mm	(USSR)	
Anti-tank	107 mm RCL	(USSR)	
	82 mm RCL	(USSR)	
	Sagger ATGW	(USSR)	
Infantry	Wide miscellany of Soviet and other weapons		

ARGENTINA

Strength: 65 000 (20 000 regular officers and NCOs)
Reserves theoretically 600 000, but likely to be much less. National Guard Reserve, 250 000. Territorial Reserve, 50 000

Military service: One year, plus nine in the active reserve, ten in the National Guard and five in the Territorial Guard

Background: The Argentinian Army is one of the few modern professional armies in South America and it regards itself as being well capable of defending the country from external attack, though it is difficult to see where that might come from. The main operational role is internal security and this has become more important since 1970 as the level of civil violence has grown rapidly. Politically the army is a major factor in the country and plays an important part in choosing and installing the government. It also undertakes some engineering development work and, through conscription, education.

Structure: Although there are corps, the operational formation is the brigade which has replaced the division. However, for the most part units operate independently particularly when engaged on internal security duties. There are integrated units of army aviation which are trained to co-operate with the ground forces and the air-portable battalions are air-lifted in air force aircraft.

4 corps
1 armoured brigade
1 mechanised brigade
4 infantry brigades
2 mountain brigades
1 airmobile brigade
5 AA battalions
1 army aviation battalion
NB Each brigade contains three battalions, one artillery and one engineer battalion

Equipment: Argentina is one of the small number of Latin American countries to have its own arms industry, and was the first to set it up. Much of the military weapon and ammunition supply comes from the home industry and only the more sophisticated and advanced equipment is imported.

The Tanque Argentino Mediano (TAM) is built in Argentina and its gun is a native development from the French 105 mm. The output of the ammunition factories is such that a good deal is exported.

AFVs Tanks	TAM	(Argentina)	
	M4 Sherman (modernised)	(USA/Argentina)	100
	AMX-13	(France)	120
APCs	M113	(USA)	240
	MOWAG Roland	(Switzerland)	150
	AMX-VCI	(France)	
SP guns	155 mm Mk F3	(France)	24
	105 mm M7	(USA)	20
	155 mm M109	(USA)	6

Artillery	155 mm	(USA)	200		106 mm RCL	(USA)
	105 mm	(USA)			SS11 ATGW	(France)
	105 mm pack				Cobra 2000 ATGW	(West Germany)
	howitzer	(Italy)			Mathogo ATGW	(Argentina)
	30, 35, 40, 90 mm			**Mortars**	81 mm Hotchkiss	
	AA guns	(Various)			Brandt	(France)
	Tigercat SAM	(UK)		**Infantry**	7.62 mm small arms of FN design and Argentinian manufacture	
Anti-tank	75 mm, 90 mm,					

AMX-13 light tanks of the Argentinian Army on parade. (C. Foss)

15

AUSTRALIA

Strength: 32 300 regular
Reserves 23 800 with training obligations
Military service: Voluntary
Background: Undoubtedly one of the most efficient armies in the world, the Australian Army is small and this must count against its effectiveness for a prolonged general war. However, for the defence of the Homeland and for small-scale offensive operations in the Pacific theatre there is no doubt that it is a force to be reckoned with and it gained an enviable reputation in Viet-Nam. The potential of the Citizen Military Forces (CMF), which is the name given to the reserve army, is also high and it could provide useful and rapidly mobilised reinforcements. The Army is very well trained and well equipped. The Leopard tanks are a recent change, and there are several orders out for missiles, both SAM and SSM.

Structure: The basic structure of the army is one regular infantry division and seven CMF field forces. One of these is earmarked to reinforce the regular division on mobilisation and the other six would be responsible for home defence. To control these latter six in peacetime there are three full-time Field Force HQs which are part of the regular Order of Battle. The general organisation of the army follows British lines and there are similarities in the training also.

1 infantry divisional HQ
3 task force HQs
1 tank regiment
2 cavalry (APC) regiments
6 infantry battalions
1 SAS regiment
4 artillery regiments (1 medium, 2 field, 1 LAA)
3 engineer regiments
1 field survey regiment
1 aviation regiment
2 signal regiments
2 transport regiments
1 logistic support force

Equipment: Australia has an indigenous, and effective, small arms industry, but for practically all other war-like equipment she is reliant on imports from other countries, mostly USA and Europe. The result is that there is a wide mixture of items, which seem to be harmoniously combined and maintained with no loss of effectiveness.

AFVs Tanks	Leopard	(West Germany)	103
APCs	M113	(USA)	750
Artillery	5.5 in guns	(UK)	34
	105 mm pack	(Italy)	253
	40 mm AA	(UK)	
	Rapier SAM	(UK)	8
Anti-tank	120 mm Wombat RCL	(UK)	
	106 mm M40 RCL	(USA)	
Infantry	Redeye SAM	(USA)	
	81 mm mortar	(UK)	
	7.62 mm M60 machine gun	(USA)	
	7.62 mm L4A4 light machine gun	(UK)	
	7.62 mm L1A1 rifle	(Australia)	

Australian troops deploying from an M113 personnel carrier. (Australian MOD/MARS)

AUSTRIA

Strength: 35 000 (10 000 regular, 25 000 conscripts) Reserves 115 000 effective. 11 250 in para-military gendarmerie

Military service: 6 months, followed by 60 days refresher training spread over 12 years. By electing to serve for 8 months the refresher training commitment is waived

Background: The Austrian Army has a long and honourable history stretching back through the Austro-Hungarian Empire, but it disappeared completely at the end of the Second World War and was slowly rebuilt under the Allied Occupation as an internal security force. Later, when the country became independent, the intention was to copy the Swiss forces but this never actually came about and the present framework was not fixed until 1970 with the decision to have a number of regular 'Alert' units backed by a substantial militia. In time this may be slowly changed to more of a Swiss model since Austria has declared that she is perpetually neutral and will defend her frontiers against violations of that neutrality.

The principal role of the army is to defend the country, and to prevent the passage of combatants through Austrian territory. By a special act of parliament volunteers may serve outside the country with the UN peacekeeping forces on a contractual basis.

Structure: There are the usual arms of the service in the army, which also includes the air force. The basic army formation is the brigade of which there are two types,

mechanised and infantry. Each brigade consists of a headquarters battalion, three combat battalions (one of which is the training unit), and an artillery battalion. In the mechanised brigade the two combat battalions are one tank and one mechanised infantry. In the infantry brigades they are both infantry. The mechanised and tank battalions have three companies each while the infantry have four, but these are not always up to strength and some units have been a company short. The artillery has three batteries to a battalion. The headquarters battalion of the brigade contains the service units, the transport signals and medical and reconnaissance companies.

There are also some independent units, though the general intention is to phase these out and integrate them into the brigades. The *Landwehr* (Territorial Reserve) is organised for frontier and local defence only. Ex-conscripts who have been trained for their 60 days over 12 years will form local defence units on mobilisation.

3 mechanised brigade HQ battalions
3 infantry brigade HQ battalions
3 tank battalions
3 mechanised infantry battalions
3 SP artillery battalions
3 mechanised training battalions
6 infantry battalions
3 artillery battalions
3 infantry training battalions

Saurer Schützenpanzer of the Austrian Army. (C. Foss)

AUSTRIA

4 AA artillery battalions
3 engineer battalions
5 signal battalions
28 *Landwehr* regiments

Equipment: The main arms manufacturer in Austria is the Steyr-Daimler-Puch combine which makes small arms, trucks and light armoured vehicles, some of native design and some licence built. Larger equipment is imported, with a preference for that made in other neutral countries.

AFVs Tanks	M60A1 (more on order)	(USA)	150	
	M47 (being replaced by M60A1)	(USA)	120	
APCs	Saurer 4K4F	(Austria)	460	
SP guns	Kürassier 105 mm SP ATk	(Austria)	120	
	155 mm M109	(USA)	38	
Artillery	155 mm M1	(USA)	24	
	105 mm M2	(USA)	106	
	130 mm Steyr 680 multiple RL	(Austria)	18	
	40 mm 55/57 Bofors AA	(Sweden)	59	
	40 mm M42 AA	(USA)		
	35 mm Oerlikon AA	(Switzerland)		
	20 mm Oerlikon AA	(Switzerland)		
Anti-tank	85 mm M52/55	(Czechoslovakia)	240	
	106 mm M40A1	(USA)	400	
Mortars	120 mm M30	(USSR)	82	
	107 mm M2	(USA)	100	
Infantry	81 mm mortar	(Austria)	300	
	84 mm Carl Gustaf RCL	(Sweden)		
	74 mm Miniman	(Sweden)		

Small arms designed and manufactured by Steyr

BAHRAIN

Strength: 2300 regular. No conscripts
No known reserves
Military service: Voluntary
Background: Bahrain became independent in 1971 and the small army is maintained solely for internal security and to assist the police if required. It has no other operational commitment and no experience other than policing internally.
Structure: There is one infantry battalion and one armoured car squadron.

Equipment: All equipment is imported and is entirely British.

AFVs Armoured cars	Saladin	(UK)	8
Scout cars	Ferret	(UK)	8
Anti-tank	120 mm Wombat		
	RCL	(UK)	8
Mortars	81 mm	(UK)	6

Bahrain uses a variety of infantry weapons including the Italian Beretta M12 SMG. (C. Foss)

21

BANGLADESH

Strength: 70 000 regular. Para-military frontier force (Bangladesh Rifles) 20 000
Armed police reserve, 36 000. No organised army reserve
Background: The Bangladesh Army has inherited many of the characteristics of the old British Army in India and it is largely organised on traditional British lines. The country became independent in 1971 after appalling bloodshed and privations. It is still the poorest country in the world with no effective budget and no proper income apart from foreign aid. The army provides a secure employment for all in it and there is a rush of volunteers for every vacancy. Morale is not high and the army played a large part in the revolt of 1975. The main role is internal security together with the administration of the country's political life. The Bangladesh Rifles patrol the frontier regions and there have been clashes with Indian troops.
Structure: Theoretically the army is divided into five divisions containing eleven brigades and some independent units. In practice it seems that the divisional grouping is more for administrative control throughout the country and the lowest practical formation is the brigade. For the most part the infantry units are spread throughout the country as a peacekeeping force. The tanks are kept at Bogra. The absence of a reserve is a political decision since it is felt that such a force can easily become a "People's Army" and attack the government.

 5 divisional HQ

11 infantry brigade HQ
33 infantry battalions
 1 tank regiment
 6 artillery regiments
 3 engineer battalions

Equipment: There is no arms industry in Bangladesh and all equipment has to be imported. The crippling shortage of money has meant that spares and ammunition are scarce and it is likely that many of the quoted weapons are no longer operational. It is known that training has been curtailed due to shortages of ammunition.

AFVs Tanks	T-34	(USSR)	30
Artillery	105 mm M2	(USA)	30
	25 pdr	(UK)	5
Anti-tank	106 mm M40 RCL	(USA)	
	6 pdr	(UK)	
Mortars	120 mm	(USSR)	50
	81 mm	(UK)	
Infantry	Various equipments, largely British and all elderly		

Right: Artillery battery of Belgian Para-Commandos. (I. V. Hogg)

BELGIUM

Strength: 62 300 (20 000 conscripts)
Reserves 600 000
Military service: 8 months if posted to West Germany, 10 months if serving in Belgium
Structure: The main contribution of the Belgian Army to NATO is 1 Belgian Corps, consisting of two divisions with a third division in the reserve army. The two active divisions are made up of roughly three quarters regular troops. The corps is fully mechanised and all the infantry are carried in APCs and the artillery is all SP. The third division is slightly smaller in total strength as the brigades have a smaller infantry content. The Para-Commandos are all regular and used as a rapid intervention force, one battalion is permanently assigned to the ACE Mobile Force.

Basic training of individual soldiers takes up most of the time that the conscript is in the service, so that there is a powerful incentive to make the army as fully regular as possible. Reserve training lasts for five years on an annual refresher basis, but after that is likely to tail off.

1 BE Corps	2 divisions (1 & 16), one in West Germany and one in Belgium
Each division	1 mechanised brigade
	1 motorised brigade
Corps troops	1 armoured brigade
	aviation squadrons
	artillery group
	engineer group

BELGIUM

			Equipment		
	recce battalions		**AFVs** Tanks	Leopard	(West Germany) 334
	logistic and communication units			AMX-13	(France)
Reserve division	1 mechanised brigade	Both slightly smaller than the		M47 (in reserve)	(USA) 62
	1 motorised brigade	regular equivalents		Scorpion	(UK) 136
				Scimitar	(UK) 154
Army troops	1 Para-Commando regiment		APCs	M75	(USA)
	3 battalions, one permanently assigned to ACEMF			Spartan	(UK) 238
				AMX-VCI	(France)

Belgian paratroops with FN AS 24 lightweight vehicles. (I. V. Hogg)

BENIN

SP guns	105 mm M108	(USA)	96
	155 mm M109	(USA)	41
	175 mm M110	(USA)	11
	90 mm JPK C-90 SP atk	(West Germany)	80
	Gepard 35 mm AA	(West Germany)	25
Artillery	203 mm towed	(USA)	15
	105 mm towed	(USA)	22
	40 mm L/70 LAA	(Sweden)	
	20 mm LAA	(West Germany)	115
	Lance SSM	(USA)	5
	M163 Vulcan LAA cannon	(USA)	
	Hawk SAM	(USA)	60
Anti-tank	106 mm M40A1 RCL	(USA)	
	ENTAC (all or nearly all now phased out)	(France)	
	MILAN ATGW	(France)	65+
	Striker with Swingfire	(UK)	44
Infantry	4.2 in mortar	(USA)	
	81 mm mortar		
	7.62 mm MAG machine gun	(Belgium)	
	7.62 mm FAL rifles	(Belgium)	

Strength: 2100. Gendarmerie 1100
There are no organised reserves
Military service: 18 months selective conscription
Background: Benin is one of the poorest countries in Africa. It became independent from France in 1960 and since then the country has suffered a succession of changes of government and internal troubles. Internal tribal stresses have been transferred to the armed forces and morale and discipline have dropped as a result. Even so, the army is probably the main cohesive factor in this country and its role is very much that of the instrument of government policy.
Structure: The army is composed of two infantry battalions, a reconnaissance squadron and an artillery battery. There is one company of what are described as para-commandos, who may well be an elite government guard force.
Equipment: All equipment has been provided by France. The armoured car squadron has a few ex-US M8s and the artillery battery has ex-French 105 mm guns.

BOLIVIA

Strength: 17 000
No apparent organised reserves. Discharged conscripts must form a pool of manpower, but the numbers are unknown

Military service: 12 months, with no clear reserve commitment

Background: The Bolivian Army, as with so many South American countries, has played a large part in the government, and still does. Its general role today is to maintain the government presence and authority throughout the country. Secondary roles are the maintenance of order in the face of organised violence by guerrilla groups and armed strikers and the safeguarding of the frontiers. There is little experience of operations in the general war sense, but the Bolivian Army conducted a brilliant campaign against Che Guevara in 1967 and finally killed him.

Structure: The country is divided into nine divisional areas with an extra division in the capital La Paz. These divisions are really convenient administrative groupings, with the additional bonus that they can conduct the annual draft. The Staff College, the NCO School and the one parachute battalion are all near to La Paz and there is no doubt that this has been done to maintain a central reserve near to the capital. The six engineer battalions operate within the interior and form the main civil engineering strength of the country. The infantry battalions are scattered throughout the divisional areas while the armour and the artillery remain at the main bases near the larger cities.

10 divisions
 4 cavalry regiments
 1 mechanised regiment
13 infantry regiments
 1 motorised regiment
 2 ranger regiments
 1 parachute battalion
 3 artillery regiments
 6 engineer battalions

Equipment: Bolivia has no arms industry and imports everything for the army. Traditionally it has bought arms from Central Europe, and this continues though on a much smaller scale than previously. Now much of the weaponry is ex-US. It is believed that the standards of maintenance and training are good.

AFVs	APCs	M113	(USA)	18
		MOWAG	(Switzerland)	20
Armoured cars		M107 Commando	(USA)	10
Artillery		105 mm FH-18	(West Germany)	20
		105 mm M101 howitzer	(USA)	25
		75 mm M116 pack howitzer	(USA)	25
		75 mm guns		6
Mortars		107 mm	(USA)	
		81 mm	(USA)	
Infantry		Small arms bought from Switzerland and West Germany		

BOTSWANA

Strength: approx 1000
No known reserves
Military service: Voluntary
Background: The Botswana Defence Force was formed in 1977 and it is hoped that it will rise to a total of 2000. Training is under way and there is an armed police force of about 1200 men. The main task of both forces is the guarding of the frontiers and internal security.

BRAZIL

Strength: 180 000 (110 000 conscripts)
Reserves. No formal reserve forces, but the State Militia of 250 000 provides a source of trained manpower
Military service: One year. Selective conscription
Background: Brazil is the largest country in South America. It occupies 43% of the land mass and has almost half the population of the continent. All except Chile and Ecuador have common frontiers with her. The country gained independence in the early nineteenth century without revolution and bloodshed, thus the army plays a less prominent part in the political life than in other nations where it was responsible for the people's colonial liberation. There is nevertheless some anxiety about frontier safety and also for internal security and government repression. The main roles of the army are firstly, to act as a moderating influence in the political life of the country and secondly to maintain the security of the frontiers. A third role, which is less prominent, is to educate the poorer conscripts and return them to civilian life as better equipped citizens. About 40% of the army is regular and these regulars form the real basis of the active army. The conscripts spend most of their one year's service in training of one kind or another and rarely contribute much to the active formations.

Regulars are very well trained and the existing schools are among the best in the world. Unusually, there is no formal system of reserves for the army and it is presumed that the State Militias would provide additional troops were they ever needed. Conscripts rarely, if ever, do any refresher training despite this being part of their commitment. Conscription is highly selective since about 1 000 000 are eligible for call-up each year, far more than are needed.

Structure: Operationally the army is divided into geographical zones with military regions inside these zones. There are four zones and eleven regions, each being responsible for recruiting and training within its areas. The divisional and brigade formations are included within these regions, the main concentration being in the more vulnerable south. Formations are well manned and the divisions can contain up to four brigades with all supporting arms and services. The Air Force has sufficient transport aircraft to lift one parachute battalion at any one time.

8 divisions, each of up to four brigades of three battalions.
Brigades are armoured, mechanised or motorised infantry
2 independent infantry brigades
1 parachute brigade
5 light infantry "jungle" battalions

Equipment: Brazil has the largest and most technically advanced arms industry in the Third World. It is continually expanding and there is no doubt that she is intending to be a major exporter of arms within a short time. Already about 40% of the army's equipment is home-produced, much of it under licence but with an increasing proportion designed and developed in Brazil. The firm of Engesa has

EE9 Cascavel now in service with the Brazilian Army. (C. Foss)

BRAZIL

an international reputation for AFVs and trucks and Avibras manufactures ammunition and rockets.

AFVs Tanks	M4	(USA)	100	
	M3A1	(USA)	250	
	M41	(USA)	250	
	X-1A2	(Brazil)	35	
APCs	M113	(USA)	600	
	EE-11 Urutu	(Brazil)		
	M59	(USA)		
Armoured cars	EE-9 Cascavel	(Brazil)	120	
	M8	(USA)		
SP guns	105 mm M108	(USA)	24	
Artillery	155 mm M114	(USA)	90	
	105 mm M7	(USA)	450	
	75 mm M116 pack howitzers	(USA)	500	

	108 mm multiple RL 108R	(Brazil)	
	180 mm triple launch rocket X20	(Brazil)	
	300 mm rocket X40	(Brazil)	
	40 mm Bofors AA	(Sweden)	30
	90 mm AA	(USA)	40
	Roland SAM	(France)	
Anti-tank	106 mm M40A1 RCL	(USA)	
	Cobra ATGW	(West Germany, made in Brazil)	
Infantry	81 mm mortars		

Most small arms are licence-built from Europe but there is a steadily increasing number of Brazilian-designed and made weapons coming into service

BRUNEI

Strength: 2500
No reserves. 1700 Police
Military service: Voluntary
Background: An independent Sultanate on the northwest coast of Borneo, Brunei remains a member of the Commonwealth with Britain responsible for defence and foreign relations. A battalion of ghurkas is stationed in the country and to supplement it there is the Royal Brunei Regiment. The main role of the army is to safeguard the frontiers, in particular the frontier with Indonesia from where several large raids were mounted during the confrontation crisis in the 1960s. Manpower is short in the country and it is not expected that the Regiment can expand to much more than 3500 men at most.
Structure: All defence forces come under the army. So far the army comprises two battalions, with the hope of raising a third. There is one armoured squadron and an engineer troop. A small boat squadron patrols the inland rivers.

2 infantry battalions
1 armoured reconnaissance squadron
1 engineer troop
1 special boat squadron

Equipment: All equipment is imported. The great majority is British, but there are signs that the Regiment is prepared to buy from other countries and the 81 mm mortars in the battalions are Israeli.

AFVs Tanks	Scorpion CVR(T)	(UK)	16
APCs	Sankey	(UK)	24
AA	Rapier SAM (on order)	(UK)	

BULGARIA

Strength: 115 000 (75 000 conscripts)
Reserves approx 200 000. In addition a People's Militia of 150 000
Military service: Two years for conscripts
Background: In 1944 the Soviet Union declared war on Bulgaria which was then fighting on the side of the Axis, and invaded shortly afterwards. Since then the country has been another communist satellite and the army was thoroughly reorganised in the early 1950s making it a model of the Soviet Army with many Soviet officers in key positions. It is now fully integrated into the Warsaw Pact and a staunch Soviet ally. The main role of the army is the maintenance of the regime and national defence, but it is also available to the Soviet Union were the Pact armies to be called out. Training is good and thorough, though the technical standards are not as high as in other Pact forces. All units are stationed inside Bulgaria and the only recent occasion when they crossed frontiers was in 1968 when some went into Czechoslovakia.
Structure: Bulgaria is unusual among the Pact forces in not forming tank divisions. The eight motor rifle divisions in the army are supported by tank regiments from the independent brigades and this is a system unique to Bulgaria. All formations are below strength, some probably down to half. The one parachute regiment is under air force command. There is probably enough air lift for one battalion in helicopters and one in parachute aircraft at any one time.

8 motor rifle divisions, each of three regiments of three battalions with supporting arms
5 tank brigades
1 parachute regiment
4 artillery regiments
3 AA regiments
3 SSM battalions
2 reconnaissance battalions

Equipment: There is scarcely any indigenous arms industry and almost every item of equipment is imported from the Soviet Union.

AFVs	Tanks	T-34	(USSR)	100
		T-54/55	(USSR)	1800
		T-62	(USSR)	few
Reconnaissance vehicles		PT-76 light tanks	(USSR)	250
		BRDM	(USSR)	250

BURUNDI

APCs	BTR-60, OT-62	(USSR)	2000
SP guns	SU-100	(USSR)	
Artillery	152 mm M55	(USSR)	90
	122 mm M55	(USSR)	400
	85 mm D-44	(USSR)	200
	122 mm BM-21 RL	(USSR)	
	Frog-7 SSM	(USSR)	36
	Scud SSM	(USSR)	20
	100 mm AA	(USSR)	
	85 mm AA	(USSR)	
	57 mm AA	(USSR)	
Anti-tank	100 mm M55 gun	(USSR)	
	85 mm M45 gun	(USSR)	
	57 mm M43 gun	(USSR)	
	82 mm B-10 RCL	(USSR)	
	Sagger ATGW	(USSR)	
	Snapper ATGW	(USSR)	
Mortars	160 mm	(USSR)	
	120 mm	(USSR)	
Infantry	82 mm mortars		
	Soviet equipment throughout		

Strength: 7000. 2000 gendarmerie. All armed forces incorporated in the army

Military service: Voluntary

Background: Burundi became independent in 1962 and since then has had a history of internal troubles coupled with a fragile and uncertain economy. There were two major revolts in 1972 and 1973 in which the army was fully involved. Since then it has concentrated on keeping the peace.

Structure: Little is known of the actual military structure, but it can be assumed that it follows the Belgian pattern. The largest formation is the battalion. The available airlift is quite insufficient for the declared airborne unit.

Equipment: Burundi has no arms industry. All equipment has been provided under aid schemes or bought.

AFVs Armoured cars	AML	(France)	
Anti-tank	75 mm RCL	(USA)	
Mortars	81 mm	(France)	

BURMA

Strength: 153 000
No formal reserves. People's Police Force, 35 000. Some local village Home Guards
Military service: Voluntary
Background: Burma gained its independence from Britain in 1948 and almost immediately was plunged into internal conflict. The newly-formed Burmese Army had to play a major part in the pacifying of the various factions within the states and at the same time became the only effective instrument of government. One policy which has remained throughout the years since independence is that of non-alignment so that no outside nation was called in to assist or to produce aid. The result is that Burma has been secluded from the world for many years and the army has become more and more a power in the political life. It now controls almost every aspect of government, the economy and business life. Operations are confined to what seems to be a perpetual running war with tribes along the borders though relations with neighbours are good and there is no immediate prospect of any other country trying to invade or to violate any national areas. The close links between the ruling party and the army mean that officers are also often members of the government and local military commanders are also party officials for that district.
The army has had a considerable degree of success against rebel movements and the country is now relatively quiet internally. All service is voluntary, and there is no

shortage of recruits. The quality of the soldiers is good and training appears to be thorough. The policy of not accepting aid has perhaps limited the ability of the army in some respects, but it remains a well-disciplined and effective force.
Structure: Because of the country's unaligned policy, the army is able to concentrate on internal security as a main priority. Units are spread around the country in nine regional commands which closely correspond with the state boundaries. The strategic reserve is formed from three infantry divisions each with three brigades, or Tactical Operation Commands (TOC) as they are known in Burma. A battalion follows the British system of organisation with four rifle companies of three platoons and a support company with mortars and machine guns. Normal strength is about 500 men, but the proper establishment calls for about 750. A TOC can accept up to four battalions, three being normal. Armour and artillery are not normally deployed unless the situation calls for them.
  3 infantry divisions
  2 armoured battalions
16 brigades (TOCs) each of three or four battalions, in nine
   regional commands
  5 artillery battalions
Equipment: The policy of both government and army is to rely on their own resources for arms or to buy from abroad, with cash if necessary. Most of the existing equipment is

British and American, but gradually the smaller and lighter arms are being replaced by those made in Burma. The local arms industry is very new and short of capital equipment, but light ammunition is now made in sufficient quantities. All heavy weapons are obsolete as are the vehicles.

AFVs Tanks	Comet	(UK)	
Armoured cars	Humber	(UK)	40
	Ferret	(UK)	45
Artillery	25 pdr	(UK)	50
	5.5 in	(UK)	
	76 mm mountain	(Yugoslavia)	120
	105 mm M2	(USA)	80
	3.7 in AA	(UK)	
	40 mm AA	(UK)	
Anti-tank	17 pdr	(UK)	50
	6 pdr	(UK)	
Mortars	120 mm Soltam	(Israel)	
Infantry	Many obsolete types, particularly ex-British. Also, West German G3 rifles and G1 machine guns, some locally made in Burma		

CAMEROON

Strength: 5500
No reserve, but a gendarmerie of 5000 could provide trained men
Military service: Mainly voluntary in the formed units, but a law requiring all fit men to undergo military training does exist
Background: Cameroon is formed from the ex-French Cameroons and parts of the old British colony. There was some serious rebellion just after independence in 1960, but it appears to have died down now. The last French garrison left in 1974. The small army is occupied in internal security and frontier surveillance. There have been many frontier incidents since Cameroon has borders with six other countries.
Structure: The army consists of four battalions, one based in each of the civil districts. The reconnaissance company seems to provide an armoured reserve and the one parachute company has been used for rapid reinforcement of the more distant frontiers. There is a small support element of engineers and signallers.
Equipment: All equipment comes from outside the country and is almost exclusively French, apart from the armoured cars.

AFVs Armoured cars	M8	(USA)
	Ferret	(UK)
Artillery	105 mm gun	(France)
	75 mm gun	(France)
Mortars	81 mm	(France)

CANADA

Strength: 28 500
Reserves 15 200
Military service: Voluntary
Background: The Canadian armed forces have an enviable reputation for hard, professional fighting ability, gained in two world wars and several lesser conflicts. The Army is now part of Mobile Command since all forces were unified in 1968. The role of the Land Forces element is fourfold, the protection of Canadian sovereignty, the defence of North America in conjunction with US forces, the fulfilment of such NATO agreements as may exist and the performance of whatever peacekeeping UN tasks Canada may assume. To perform these wide-ranging roles Mobile Command keeps a large percentage of the Land Forces in Canada, spread around the country. Their main tasks are both training and internal security together with general frontier surveillance. A mechanised brigade group in West Germany fulfils the NATO commitment, together with an air-mobile battalion earmarked for the AMF(L). In addition, there are several UN peacekeeping commitments in different parts of the world, the largest being in Cyprus where there is a battalion.

All recruitment is voluntary and training is of a high quality, often conducted at schools which cater for all the armed services together. Reserve troops are held in the Militia which is a force closely linked to the regular formations. The Militia covers all arms and services and is formed into battalions which would reinforce the regular formations as complete units in time of war.

Structure: The army is currently divided into four formations, three of them in Canada and one in West Germany. In Alberta one brigade group commands units spread right across western Canada. In the east another brigade group based in Quebec covers to the Atlantic. In Ontario there is the Special Service Force, a unique organisation which is a small brigade intended as a quick-reaction force. All the units are either air-portable or air-droppable, though the number of aircraft which would be available at any one time is problematical and would limit operations. These Canadian-based formations are stationed in locations which are largely traditional military posts and they do not necessarily follow any hard and fast tactical or strategic plan. There has been criticism in Canada of the fact that these formations are not up to strength and all of them rely on their reserves making them up before being committed to action, but this is a difficulty which is not restricted to Canada alone.

2 brigade groups, each consisting of
  1 armoured regiment
  1 artillery regiment
  3 infantry battalions
  1 engineer regiment
  HQ and supporting troops
1 mechanised brigade

Canadian Snowmobile mounting .5-in machine gun. (I. V. Hogg)

1 armoured regiment
1 SP artillery regiment
2 infantry battalions
HQ and supporting troops
1 Special Service Force
  1 armoured regiment
  1 artillery regiment
  1 airborne infantry regiment
  1 air-portable infantry battalion
  HQ and supporting troops

Equipment: Canada has a small arms industry and makes a fair proportion of its needs in Canada. Much of the manufacture is licence building of foreign designs and this has been successful enough to allow for a modest flow of exports, particularly to USA. Attempts to design and build artillery and AFVs proved to be too expensive for the budget to absorb and now all of these are either bought outright or made in Canada with modifications to suit the particular needs of the forces.

AFVs	Tanks	Leopard C-1	(West Germany)	114
	Reconnaissance vehicles	Lynx	(USA)	175
		Cougar	(Switzerland/ Canada)	174 on order
	APCs	M113	(USA)	800
		Grizzly	(Switzerland/ Canada)	300 on order
	SP guns	155 mm M109A	(USA)	50
Artillery		105 mm C1	(USA/Canada)	170
		105 mm L-5 pack	(Italy)	57
		40 mm Bofors AA	(Sweden)	40
		Blowpipe SAM	(UK)	100
Anti-tank		TOW ATGW	(USA)	150
Infantry		81 mm mortars	(UK)	
		84 mm Carl Gustaf RCL	(Sweden)	
		7.62 mm Browning M1919A1 GPMG	(USA)	
		7.62 mm C1 Rifle	(Canada)	
		9 mm C1 SMG	(Canada)	

TOW on Canadian M113.

CENTRAL AFRICAN REPUBLIC

Strength: 1100
No known reserves, but a gendarmerie of 1400 can provide a pool of trained manpower
Military service: Two years
Background: The CAR is best known for the extravagant and ruinous coronation of the one-time Emperor Bokassa. It gained independence from France in 1960 and since then has remained a poor and backward country heavily dependent on France. The Army is both small and indifferently trained. For some years its main task was the guarding of the presidential palace and frequent repressions of popular feeling among the population. It cannot be considered to be an effective force.
Structure: The army is only one infantry battalion, with small engineer and signals attachments
Equipment: Most is ex-French (and in itself may be ex-US in origin) though occasional Chinese and Soviet weapons have been identified.

CHAD

Strength: 4500. Para-military forces, 6000
No formal reserves
Military service: Three years, on a rather random system of conscription
Background: Chad is another ex-French colony which became independent in 1960. Since then it has had a troubled history and the government has fought a constant internal war against the Moslem FROLINAT rebellion. France has renounced all formal links with Chad, though it is suspected that she still largely props up both government and army. The training of the army is French and there has been some slight US and Israeli assistance.
Structure: The army consists of three infantry battalions with a fourth being formed. Some of the infantry companies are para-trained and used for rapid reinforcement and independent operations.
3 infantry battalions
1 armoured car squadron
Equipment: Practically all equipment is French.

AFVs Armoured cars	AML	(France)
Mortars	120 mm	(France)
	81 mm	(France)

CHILE

Strength: 50 000 (20 000 conscripts)
Reserves 160 000. Para-military forces, 30 000 armed police (Carabineiros)
Military service: One year
Background: After a long history of non-intervention in political affairs, the army overthrew the Allende government in 1973 and since then has played a leading part in the ruling of the country. In the 1900s the army was set up on Prussian lines and this influence is still visible in many ways. Training is good and particularly officer training. The army is not committed to any external role and is now used for the retention of internal law and order together with the defence of the national territory. There are continual disputes over frontiers. 60% of the army is composed of regular soldiers and the conscripts are largely selected by lottery. A major objective of conscription is to combat the low educational levels among much of the population. Conscript training is done within units, which must constitute a burden on the officers and NCOs.

Structure: There are six divisions which are deployed on a territorial rather than an operational basis. Divisional strength probably varies slightly but is often quoted as being of four infantry regiments together with an armoured regiment and one or two artillery regiments, together with supporting services. The five military instructional schools could each field a well-trained formation made up from the staff. There is insufficient logistical support for a viable campaign outside Chile, but the army is well able to defend the country against incursions. The reserves receive scarcely any refresher training and must be a doubtful asset.

 6 divisional HQ
 3 armoured regiments
 3 cavalry regiments
20 infantry regiments (most of three battalions, but some have less. Number includes nine motorised regiments and three mountain regiments)
 6 artillery regiments
 Miscellaneous AA and support detachments

Equipment: The only military manufacturing appears to be in the field of ammunition. All other weapons and hardware are imported, mostly from Europe and USA. A small quantity of Soviet weapons were imported during the Allende presidency and these, together with captured stocks from guerrilla organisations, introduce a complicating factor in the equipment tables.

AFVs Tanks	M4 medium	(USA)	75
	M3 light	(USA)	10
	M41	(USA)	60
	AMX-13 light	(France)	47
Armoured cars	EE-9 Cascavel	(Brazil)	30
APCs	M113	(USA)	300
	MOWAG MR-8	(Switzerland)	

Artillery	105 mm M101	(USA)	
	105 mm M56 pack	(USA)	36
	40 mm Bofors AA	(USA)	
Anti-tank	106 mm M40A1 RCL	(USA)	
Mortars	120 mm Brandt	(France)	
	81 mm M1	(USA)	
Infantry	7.62 mm FN machine guns	(Belgium)	
	7.62 mm MG42 machine guns	(West Germany)	
	7.62 mm rifles	(Belgium)	
	7.62 mm SIG rifles	(Switzerland)	

Chile has recently taken delivery of a quantity of French AMX-30 MBTs. (C. Foss)

CHINA PEOPLE'S REPUBLIC

Strength: 3 250 000

Reserves. The entire population of military age can be considered a reserve, but in practical terms the available pool of trained manpower lies in the Armed Militia which is between 5 000 000 and 7 000 000 in strength

Military service: Two to four years. Conscription is selective and only about 10% of the draft is actually called into the army. The remainder are automatically sent to the Militia for the same period of time. A large element of the army is regular.

Background: It is difficult for western minds to imagine the size of China and the enormous numbers of men and women involved in the military forces. The Army alone has more than three times the number of men available to all NATO. Until quite recently this huge force was intended to fight a 'People's War' which was defined as a mixture of guerrilla and human wave tactics, based on an elastic defence and almost entirely lacking in offensive capability. This is slowly being changed. The offensive strike force of the nuclear troops is retained, but the army is slowly being more extensively equipped and will in time be able to move more readily and fight more flexibly. At present movement is restricted to the railways with local movement entirely on foot. Any military operation of more than a minor size requires a large dumping programme and it is not possible to make other than very minor alterations to tactical plans. The invasion of northern Viet-Nam in 1979

undoubtedly used the few fully equipped divisions which are capable of independent operations and are properly equipped with transport and armour. Even then the results were not too impressive, underlining the fact that the People's Liberation Army (PLA) is really only suited to defence and not offence.

Another factor limiting the offensive capability of the PLA must be lack of experience. Apart from the Vietnamese operation there has been no actual experience of war since Korea and that was no real basis on which to build a doctrine for modern war. In any case, the PLA plays a different part in Chinese life than do most other armies, perhaps the best way to illustrate this is to quote in full the relevant article of the Constitution which lays down the tasking for the army.

"The Chinese People's Liberation Army is at all times a fighting force, and simultaneously a working force and a production force. The task of the armed forces of the People's Republic of China is to safeguard the achievement of the socialist revolution and socialist construction, to defend the sovereignty and security of the State, and to guard against subversion and aggression by imperialism, social imperialism and their lackeys."

From this it is clear that the army does much more than act as a purely military force. It plays a large part in production and construction work, particularly those projects requiring massive quantities of labour and it is used for political

tasks such as indoctrination and education. The training of regulars places great emphasis on political and psychological aspects while actual military training is inclined to be quite basic. It seems that large scale exercises are never held, nor is there much live firing due to continual and chronic ammunition shortages. On the other hand, fitness training is very good and all soldiers are capable of long marches with full kit. Senior commanders are trained on models and map exercises, which are good for teaching the main skills, but are no substitute for taking men into the field.

Structure: The deployment of regular troops has changed little in the last 20 years. There are about 1 000 000 men in the areas near to the Soviet and Mongolian borders, the likely breakdown of formations being a mix of regular and supporting divisions. The remainder of the PLA is spread throughout the country more or less evenly with a noticeable concentration opposite Taiwan and again near to Peking. A strategic reserve of the more mobile divisions is usually kept in the northern half of the country where they could best cope with any overland incursion over the sensitive Soviet frontier. The whole country is divided into eleven Military Regions (MR) within which are Military Districts (MD). Both are capable of operating as independent military commands in war.

The PLA is divided into armies. An army consists of several corps and may have an armoured division under command of the army commander. A corps consists of three divisions and may have an artillery division attached. A division consists of three regiments of three battalions, an artillery regiment and supporting arms and services; it might have a tank regiment attached if it is an infantry division. An armoured division is likely to have two tank regiments and an infantry regiment, the latter motorised or in APCs. There are also many independent formations and units, mainly of regimental strength, under the direct command of a MD. These formations are organised on the same lines as the divisions, but their equipment is lighter and, though there is some artillery for them, there are no tanks and very few armoured vehicles of any kind.

The Militia are given basic training and are armed with small arms only. They are organised into infantry companies and are responsible for local defence.

Engineer, railway and transport troops of the regular army are organised into divisions of which there are more than 40.

- 11 armoured divisions
- 115 infantry divisions
- 3 airborne divisions
- 40 artillery divisions
- 150 independent regimental formations
- 40+ engineer, railway and construction divisions
  Local forces consisting of up to 80 infantry divisions and 130 independent regiments

Equipment: By the standards of western armies the PLA is seriously under-equipped. The most acute shortage is in motor transport and armoured vehicles. This deficiency is slowly being overcome, but the requirements are enormous and it will take some time before there is enough for all formations. There is an indigenous arms industry which produces copies or adaptations of Soviet designs. Production now embraces all types of vehicle and weapon, including tanks, artillery pieces and ammunition. There is a marked lack of sophisticated equipment such as night-driving aids and radar, but the essential features are all adequately designed and built and indeed the general impression is similar to that of Soviet equipment in the early 1960s when the emphasis was on ruggedness and reliability rather than complication. It can be expected that weapons will stay in service for much longer in China than in other countries simply because of the huge quantities needed for a replacement programme.

AFVs	Tanks	MBT (based on T-62)	(PRC)	
		T-59	(PRC)	
		Type 60	(PRC)	10,000
		Type 62 light	(PRC)	
APCs		K-3	(PRC)	1,500

Artillery	152 mm gun/how	(USSR)	
	130 mm gun	(USSR)	
	122 mm gun/how	(USSR)	
	SU-76	(USSR)	16,000
	SU-85	(USSR/PRC)	
	SU-100 SP guns	(USSR/PRC)	
	SU-122	(USSR/PRC)	
	140 mm BM-14 RL	(USSR)	
	132 mm BM-13 RL	(USSR)	
	107 mm Type 63 RL	(PRC)	
Anti-tank	85 mm Type 56 gun	(PRC)	
	76 mm Type 54 gun	(PRC)	
	57 mm Type 55 gun	(PRC)	
	90 mm Type 65 RCL	(PRC)	
	75 mm Type 56 RCL	(PRC)	
	57 mm Type 52 RCL	(PRC)	
	MILAN and HOT ATGW	(France) (on order)	
Mortars	160 mm	(PRC)	
	120 mm Type 53	(PRC)	
	82 mm Type 53	(PRC)	
Infantry	All infantry weapons in service are copies of Soviet designs with the exception of the following which are native Chinese designs.		
	7.62 mm Type 68 rifle		
	7.62 mm Type 67 machine gun		

COLOMBIA

Strength: 50 000
Reserves 250 000-300 000
Military service: Two years. Ex-conscripts remain in the reserve until aged 45
Background: The Colombian Army probably has more operational experience than any other in South America. It has fully supported the United Nations and has sent troops to several peacekeeping missions. It also maintained an infantry battalion in Korea during the 1950-53 war. Since 1948 it has contained a serious internal security threat within its own country and there is continual activity against guerrilla groups in the mountains. The state of training of the army is good and conscripts are sent to Branch schools rather than trained in units so that the operational efficiency of the unit is not affected by constant recruit instruction. This is unusual in South America. Again, unusually, the army plays only a very small part in politics and has no history of interference in government. As a result it is able to concentrate on its main task of ensuring internal stability.
Structure: The brigades are all infantry and are usually stationed in the ten military regions in the country. Each one has at least two battalions with the usual quota of supporting arms and services. It seems likely that the ranger and airborne battalions form a central reserve capable of being quickly moved to trouble spots.

10 infantry brigades
 1 battalion Presidential Guard
 1 ranger battalion
 1 airborne battalion (more forming)
 1 AA artillery battalion
20 mechanised infantry battalions
 5 mechanised artillery battalions
 6 engineer battalions
Equipment: Practically all military equipment is imported, though small arms ammunition is made locally. The main suppliers have been USA and France and much of the existing equipment is elderly. There is no army aviation, but the Air Force has about 50 helicopters which are largely used for internal security duties.

AFVs Tanks	M4A3 medium	(USA)
	M3A1 light	(USA)
Armoured cars	M8	(USA)
	M20	(USA)
	M3 Half-track	(USA)
Artillery	105 mm M101 gun	(USA)
	40 mm AA	(Sweden/USA)
Infantry	7.62 mm M49/56 rifle	(France)
	7.62 mm G3 rifle	(West Germany)
	9 mm Madsen SMG	(Denmark)
	9 mm Walther MP-K	(West Germany)

9 mm Walther MP-K SMG used by Colombia. (C. Foss)

CONGO

Strength: 6500
No organised reserves, but 1400 gendarmerie and 2500 militia are spread throughout the country
Military service: Voluntary
Background: The country achieved independence in 1960 and since then has lived in a continual internal turmoil. In addition to tribal differences there are political alignments and the police distrusts the Army. Half the population lives in towns and the conditions are ripe for riot and revolt. In all this the Army could not be relied upon to support the government. In the event of war it could scarcely offer any form of effective resistance.
Structure: So far as is known the Army consists of a small number of individual units.
1 armoured regiment
1 infantry battalion
1 'Paracommando' battalion
  Small armoured car, artillery and engineer units
Equipment: Everything is imported and the state of readiness is not known, but cannot be high. Skilled maintenance men do not exist.

AFVs Tanks	Type 62	(PRC)	12
	PT-76	(USSR)	4
Armoured cars	BRDM	(USSR)	
	BTR-152	(USSR)	24
Artillery	122 mm	(USSR)	
	100 mm	(USSR)	
	75 mm	(France)	
Anti-tank	6 pdr	(UK)	
	57 mm	(USSR)	
Mortars	120 mm	(USSR)	

COSTA RICA

Strength: There is no Army, but an armed Civil Guard numbers about 3000 men with a large number of possible reserves, for whom equipment may not be fully available. The Civil Guard is organised and equipped on military lines using United States equipment and weapons, but it is not a military force and is controlled by the Minister of Public Security. The standard of training is extremely good and is among the best in South America with at least 10% of the Guard going abroad for specialist training.

CUBA

Strength: 160 000
Reserves 90 000
Military service: Three years, followed by an unknown length of time in the reserve
Background: Although a Cuban Army of sorts has existed since 1908 the present one dates from Castro's accession to power in 1959. It has progressively modernised and improved and since 1970 it has been organised on Soviet lines. Although formal training facilities appear to be few the Cuban Army now has extensive experience of actual battle, almost all on the African continent, and must rank among the better forces in the South American area. It lacks sufficient heavy equipment and armoured vehicles to be a truly modern force, and seems to rely heavily on Soviet 'advisers' to operate much of its sophisticated weaponry, however it is well organised and relatively efficient.

Structure: Within Cuba the Army is divided into three main field army areas, East, Centre and West and in each there is a recruit training centre for conscripts. Operationally the largest formation is a brigade, but these brigades are more likely to be nearly as strong as a Soviet motor rifle division, less the armoured regiments and with less artillery. The Cuban armoured regiment probably has two tank battalions. It is thought that complete brigades are deployed in Africa, though there are small detachments of 'advisers' in many of the smaller African countries.

15 infantry brigades
 3 armoured regiments
 8 independent infantry regiments (battalion groups)

CUBA

Equipment: There is no indigenous arms industry except for some manufacture of small arms ammunition and all weapons and equipment are imported from the USSR.

AFVs				
Tanks	Js-2 (obsolete)	(USSR)	60	
	T-34	(USSR)		
	T-54	(USSR)	150	
	T-55	(USSR)		
	T-62	(USSR)	50	
	PT-76	(USSR)		
Armoured cars	BRDM	(USSR)		
APCs	BTR-40/60/152	(USSR)	400	
SP guns	SU-100	(USSR)	100	

Artillery	152 mm M37	(USSR)	
	130 mm M54	(USSR)	
	122 mm M31/M55/		
	M38	(USSR)	
	105 mm M101	(USA)	
	75 mm M116	(USA)	
	Frog-4 SSM	(USSR)	30
	37 mm to 100 mm		
	guns AA	(USSR)	
	SA-2 SAM	(USSR)	
	SA-3 SAM	(USSR)	
Anti-tank	85 mm M45	(USSR)	
	57 mm M43	(USSR)	
	Snapper ATGW	(USSR)	
Mortars	82 mm M42	(USSR)	
Infantry	All weapons of Soviet origin		

CYPRUS (Greek-Cypriot)

Strength: 10 000. Declining gradually
Reserves probably in excess of 20 000
Military service: Two years
Background: The Greek Cypriot National Guard was formed in the late 1960s and since then has steadily dropped in numbers. Its role is the defence of the Greek-Cypriot part of Cyprus and the control of the many irregular groups which operate in that area. In fact it is incapable of resisting the Turkish Army should it choose to invade again, and the security of the country is very much in the hands of the United Nations Force which monitors the frontier.
Structure: The National Guard is a predominantly infantry force armed with the same weapons as the Greek Army, however there is a residue of elderly armoured vehicles left over from the pre-invasion army bolstered by a few more provided from Greece.
20 infantry units (under-strength battalions)
 1 armoured unit
 2 mechanised infantry units
  Artillery and support units
Equipment: Cyprus produces none of its military requirements and all equipment is imported. The state of readiness of the weapons and vehicles is not known.

AFVs Tanks	T-34	(USSR)	24
APCs	BTR-50	(USSR)	
Armoured cars	Marmon-Herrington	(UK)	30

Artillery	105 mm M101	(USA)	
	100 mm M44	(USSR)	
	25 pdr	(UK)	120
	75 mm M116	(USA)	
	3.7 in AA	(UK)	
	40 mm AA	(UK)	
Anti-tank	106 mm M40A1 RCL	(USA)	

CYPRUS (Turkish-Cypriot)

Strength: 5000
Military service: 2½ years
Background: The Turkish-Cypriot Security Force is a lightly armed force which might almost be described as being para-military in concept. It is scarcely intended to fight since the Turkish Army maintains a substantial force on the island and this would undertake any operations. The Security Force acts as a gendarmerie and a training ground for the young men of the population.
Structure: The Force is believed to be organised into battalions closely resembling those of the Turkish Army.
Equipment: The Force only has light arms and equipment and relies on the Army to provide all support. Indeed the Force wears the same uniform and differs only in its capbadge.

CZECHOSLOVAKIA

Strength: 140 000 (about 93 000 conscripts)
Reserves. About 300 000 army reservists. Men retain a liability for reserve service until aged 50
Background: The Czechoslovak Army was formed on Soviet lines in 1952 and this influence was reinforced after the 1968 purge. It is now undoubtedly subjected to heavy Soviet supervision and in the event of war would act as one of the Warsaw Pact armies controlled by a Soviet Headquarters. The main task of the army in peacetime is the defence of the country, and West Germany is seen as the main enemy; a secondary task is the maintenance of internal security. The state of training is good and units are well-equipped with modern arms and vehicles.

Czech airborne troops exercising with an OT-64A APC.

Structure: Formations and units are close copies of the Soviet pattern, though they are unlikely to be at full strength in peacetime. It is likely that the majority of troops are stationed in the Prague District with the intention of safeguarding the Western frontier. Soviet forces are all in Eastern Czechoslovakia.

5 tank divisions
5 motor rifle divisions
1 airborne regiment
3 artillery brigades with Scud SSM
1 anti-tank brigade
2 artillery brigades
2 AA artillery brigades

Equipment: Czechoslovakia is a highly industrialised country with an active arms industry manufacturing all types of weapons and vehicles up to the size of APCs and SP guns. Much of this is exported to other WP countries and friendly Middle Eastern governments. Within Czechoslovakia maintenance standards are high.

AFVs	Tanks	T-54/55	(USSR)	
		T-62	(USSR)	3400
		PT-76	(USSR)	
	Armoured cars	OT-65/66	(Czechoslovakia)	700
	APCs	OT-62/64/810	(Czechoslovakia)	2000
		BMP	(USSR)	300

SP guns	122 mm M-1973/4	(USSR)	
	122 mm wheeled,	(Czechoslovakia)	
	designation not known		
Artillery	152 mm D-20/ML-20	(USSR)	120
	130 mm M46	(USSR)	
	122 mm D-30/M-30	(USSR)	700
	100 mm M55	(USSR)	150
	122 mm M72 RL	(Czechoslovakia)	300
	130 mm M51 RL	(Czechoslovakia)	
	Frog SSM	(USSR)	40
	Scud SSM	(USSR)	30
	SA-4/6/7 SAM	(USSR)	
Anti-tank	57 mm, 85 mm, 100 mm guns	(USSR)	
	Sagger, Snapper ATGW	(USSR)	
Mortars	120 mm M43	(USSR)	
	82 mm M37	(USSR)	
Infantry	Predominantly Czechoslovak designed and manufactured, but firing Soviet calibres of ammunition		

DENMARK

Strength: 22 000 (8000 + conscripts)
Reserves 75 000. (Field Army Reserve 41 000. Local Defence Forces 24 000. Others 10 000). Home Guard 55 000
Military service: 9 months plus further 5 years in the reserve
Background: The peacetime role of the Danish Army is one of general surveillance of the country's frontiers. In war it would form a part of the NATO Command and operate within that framework. NATO exercises are held on Danish territory and there is enthusiastic co-operation with several NATO armies on a bilateral basis. One infantry battalion is permanently assigned to the UN peacekeeping forces, otherwise all units remain inside Danish territory. The island of Bornholm is treated as a separate entity and only Danish troops are permitted on it.
Structure: The operational areas of Denmark are two Commands, Western and Eastern with a separate Bornholm Region. Operationally the Army is divided into a Field Army, which would operate with NATO, and the Local Defence Forces which would be responsible for home defence within the national frontiers.

The Field Army is in further two parts, the Covering Force and the Field Army Reserve. The Covering Force consists of five small armoured infantry brigades, an armoured infantry battalion, a tank battalion and an artillery battalion. This Covering Force would be augmented on mobilisation by a company to each unit. A further reserve could add an armoured and a motorised infantry battalion to each brigade.
The Local Defence Forces are entirely reservists who do only a few days training in each year and are equipped for defensive operations with little mobility. The Home Guard is a voluntary organisation armed largely with small arms.

  5 armoured brigade HQ
  5 tank battalions
10 mechanised infantry battalions
  1 independent infantry battalion (Bornholm)
  5 artillery battalions
  5 engineer companies
  1 independent reconnaissance battalion
  3 independent reconnaissance squadrons
some independent motorised infantry battalions

Centurion Mk 5/2 of the Danish Army.

DENMARK

Equipment: Although a considerable manufacturer of arms in the past, Denmark now makes hardly any and the majority of the equipment for the Army is imported, even to the extent of leasing rifles from West Germany until the NATO Small Arms Trials are ended.

AFVs Tanks	Centurion	(UK)	200
	Leopard I	(West Germany)	120
	M41	(USA)	48
APCs	M113	(USA)	630
	M106	(USA)	68
SP guns	155 mm M109	(USA)	72
Artillery	203 mm M115	(USA)	12
	155 mm M59/M114	(USA)	96
	105 mm M101	(USA)	144
	Honest John SSM	(USA)	
	40 mm L/70 AA	(Sweden)	
	Redeye SAM	(USA)	
Anti-tank	106 mm M40A1 RCL	(USA)	250
	TOW ATGW	(USA)	
Mortars	120 mm M-50	(France)	
	81 mm M/57	(Denmark)	

DOMINICAN REPUBLIC

Strength: 11 000
Gendarmerie of approximately 10 000
Military service: Voluntary. There is theoretical conscription for one year, but the armed forces are fully established with regulars
Background: The Dominican Republic has a traditional suspicion of Haiti, which has a common border with the Republic, and the main task of the Army is to maintain the security of this frontier. A secondary task is the maintenance of internal order, though this is generally left to the gendarmerie. The Army has had little experience of actual war, but it is reasonably well trained and equipped and has easily repelled some attempts to land guerrillas on the coast.
Structure: The country is divided into three military regions, North, South and West. The principal combat units are the three infantry brigades, but most military units are spread around the country in small groups, based on villages and towns.
3 infantry brigades (3 to 5 battalions in each)

1 mixed armoured battalion
1 mountain infantry battalion
1 parachute battalion (probably no larger than one company)
1 Presidential Guard battalion
1 artillery regiment
1 AA artillery regiment
1 armoured reconnaissance squadron
Equipment: The arsenal of San Cristobal is capable of producing light weapons and their ammunition as well as rebuilding heavier weapons. However, all major items come from abroad and there is a fair mixture of nationalities among the total.

AFVs Tanks	AMX-13	(France)	20
Armoured cars	AML	(France)	
	Lynx	(Canada)	20
APCs	M3	(USA)	
Artillery	105 mm M101	(USA)	
	75 mm M116	(USA)	
	40 mm Bofors AA	(Sweden)	

ECUADOR

Strength: 17 500
Reserves approximately 50 000
Military service: Two years, selective conscription
Background: The army has always taken a large part in the political life of Ecuador but by the constitution it is charged with the defence of the country and the maintenance of internal security. There is a history of border clashes with neighbouring states and with guerrillas operating inside the country.
Structure: The country is divided into six military zones, but the main concentration of the army is around the capital, Quito. The infantry battalions and independent companies are stationed in the provinces. The largest operational formation is the battalion, but brigades could probably be formed if required. Training is reasonably good.

 9 infantry battalions
 2 motor infantry battalions
 1 parachute battalion
10 independent infantry companies

1 Presidential Guard company
3 reconnaissance squadrons
4 horsed cavalry squadrons
3 artillery groups
2 engineer battalions

Equipment: Ecuador apparently manufactures no arms or ammunition and the majority of the equipment is American, though recently some French items have been bought. It is considered to be among the better-equipped South American armies.

AFVs	Tanks	AMX-13	(France)	90
		M3	(USA)	40
		M41	(USA)	25
	Armoured cars	AML-60/90	(France)	27
	APCs	M113	(USA)	20
		AMX-VC1	(France)	
	SP guns	155 mm Mk F3	(France)	6
Artillery		105 mm M101	(USA)	18
		40 mm Bofors AA	(Sweden)	10

Swiss SIG SG540 rifle used by Ecuador.

EGYPT

Strength: 300 000
Reserves, about 500 000. Para-military forces, about
120 000
Military service: Three years selective conscription
Background: Since 1952 the Egyptian Army has existed for
the sole purpose of eradicating Israel. The recent Peace
Treaty and the softening of attitudes towards the traditional enemy has brought about a change in the operational planning for the armed forces and it now appears
that Egypt is forming more mobile intervention forces for
use in other African countries and along the more distant
frontiers to the west and south of the country. The 1973
war showed that the Army could fight well, though at that
time the Higher Command proved to be too slow and
ponderous to cope with a mobile war. The concentration
on Israel was extremely expensive and it absorbed about
30% of the GNP up to 1974. The huge expenditure is now
being reduced to more moderate levels and the size of the
Army is being steadily shrunk in proportion. Training is
thorough and comprehensive for all ranks and the army is
the most effective and competent in the entire northern
half of the continent.

Structure: The basic tactical organisations are the division
and the brigade, but there are three corps which control
specific areas. 1 Corps covers the lower Nile and delta with
responsibility to the western frontier. It also controls the
main training centres. 2 and 3 Corps hold the northern and
southern halves of the Israeli front.
2 armoured divisions (each with one armoured, two
    mechanised and one artillery brigade)
3 mechanised infantry divisions (each with two
    mechanised and one artillery brigade)
5 infantry divisions (each of two brigades)
    Republican Guard Brigade (divisional strength)
3 independent armoured brigades
7 independent infantry brigades
2 airmobile brigades
2 parachute brigades
6 commando groups
6 artillery brigades
2 heavy mortar brigades
2 ATGW brigades
2 SSM regiments

Egyptian mechanised infantry in Soviet supplied BMP-1.

EGYPT

Equipment: There is an arms industry which produces small arms and minor spare parts for existing weapons and equipment. Some armoured vehicles have also been built, but in general the attempts to manufacture the heavier items have been unsuccessful. Ammunition is made in the four ordnance factories.

AFVs Tanks	T-54/55	(USSR)	850
	T-62	(USSR)	750
	PT-76	(USSR)	80
Armoured cars	BRDM 1/2	(USSR)	300
APCs	BMP-1	(USSR)	200
	OT-62/64	(Czechoslovakia)	
	BTR-40/50/60/152	(USSR)	2500
	Walid	(Egypt)	
SP guns	152 mm ISU-152	(USSR)	200
	100 mm SU-100	(USSR)	

Artillery	180 mm, 152 mm, 130 mm, 122 mm, 100 mm, 76 mm guns	(USSR)	1300
	122 mm, 132 mm, 140 mm, 240 mm RL	(USSR)	300
	Frog-4 SSM	(USSR)	30
	Scud-B Samlet	(USSR)	24
	ZSU-23, ZSU-57 AA	(USSR)	350
	Crotale SAM	(France)	20
Anti-tank	Sagger, Swatter, Milan, Swing-fire ATGW		1000
Mortars	240 mm, 160 mm, 120 mm	(USSR)	300

NB Some US equipment is being bought. A few M113 APCs may be in service

EL SALVADOR

Strength: 6000 approximately
Reserves, up to 30 000
Military service: Voluntary, with very limited conscription
Background: The present unsettled conditions in El Salvador may well have changed the military position, but the army has always been a strong force, and it is likely to have survived without much alteration. Because it offers good pay and conditions the army has always been popular as an employer, and the annual conscription intake usually only undertakes part-time reserve training. There is a military academy for officer training and several arms schools. The army is deployed in three zones throughout the country, and it has given a good account of itself in border clashes with Honduras.

Structure: A predominantly infantry force, the largest operational formation would appear to be the battalion.
3 infantry brigades (each with two battalions)
1 artillery brigade (under strength)
1 mixed armour battalion
1 AA battalion
1 parachute company
2 ranger companies
  Engineer and support companies
Equipment: El Salvador has no arms industry and employs almost entirely US equipment.

AFVs	Tanks	AMX-13 light	(France)	12
		M3 light	(USA)	3
APCs		UR-416	(West Germany)	20
Artillery		105 mm M101 howitzer	(USA)	30

ETHIOPIA

Strength: 250 000 approximately
Military service: Normally voluntary, but now boosted by conscription
Background: The heavy fighting with Eritrea and Somalia has radically changed the Ethiopian Army and it is difficult to be precise about anything at the moment. It is highly likely that most of the suitable manpower in the country is conscripted in one way or another, though not necessarily into the ranks of the army. There are several hundred Soviet 'advisers' and up to 15 000 Cubans in Ethiopia. The fighting ability of the Ethiopian Army is uncertain.
Structure: It is difficult to be certain of any facts, but the last quoted position indicated that the army is a predominantly infantry force organised on Soviet lines and equipped with Soviet equipment to a great extent.
6-12 infantry divisions
1 mechanised division
1 light division (with two parachute brigades which are probably not fully airborne trained)
Equipment: Despite the preponderance of Soviet equipment, there is still much ex-US hardware in Ethiopia, though its efficiency must be declining rapidly in the absence of spares and skilled maintenance. All equipment is imported.

AFVs	Tanks	M60	(USA)	60 approx
		T-34	(USSR)	100
		T-54/55	(USSR)	500 approx
		M41 light	(USA)	60 approx
	Armoured cars	BRDM-2	(USSR)	
		V-150 Commando	(USA)	12
	APCs	M113	(USA)	70 approx
		BTR-40/60	(USSR)	500 approx
		BMP-1	(USSR)	60 approx
	SP guns	155 mm M109	(USA)	12 approx
Artillery		152 mm D-1		
		130 mm M46	} (USSR)	100
		122 mm M30		approx
		122 mm BM-21 RL	(USSR)	
		ZSU-23/57 AA	(USSR)	
		SA-2/3/7 SAM	(USSR)	
Anti-tank		Sagger ATGW	(USSR)	
Mortars		4.2 in M2	(USA)	260
Infantry		Largely Soviet models		

FIJI

Strength: 750
Military service: Voluntary
Background: The Fijian military forces consist of one infantry battalion, manned by long-service regular soldiers who are well trained and highly capable. A territorial reserve appears to provide men on demand and the Fijian element of the UNIFIL peacekeeping force in Lebanon has a proportion of territorials who have volunteered for active service for a limited period. The Fijian army uses British equipment and methods.

FINLAND

Strength: 34 000 (28 000 conscripts)
Reserves approximately 700 000 for all three services. 30 000 are re-trained each year
Background: Finland is a strictly neutral country with her armed forces limited by Treaty to 42 000. The army cannot do more than offer resistance at the frontiers since it is forbidden to operate outside the country. However, the large reserves and the nature of the people would almost certainly bring about a repeat of the spirited 1940 defence if any neighbour were to invade. The army is well trained, although conscripts only serve for 8 months with the active army, but all citizens take a pride in their physical fitness. The army is a willing member of the various UN peacekeeping forces.
Structure: The country is divided into seven military areas, each with a brigade stationed in it. In addition there are six independent infantry battalions which are either posted to difficult areas such as Lapland or are along the coast.

Equipment: Finland manufactures and exports small arms, ammunition and light weapons and vehicles. Tampella mortars have been famous for 50 years, but heavier equipment is imported, mainly from the USSR, though Tampella also modify and adapt artillery pieces.

AFVs	Tanks	T-54/55	(USSR)
		PT-76	(USSR)
APCs		BTR-50P	(USSR)

Artillery	152 mm m/34	(Finland/USSR)
	150 mm m/40	(Finland)
	130 mm M-46	(USSR)
	122 mm M-60	(Finland)
	122 mm D-30	(USSR)
	105 mm M-37 and M-61	(Finland)
	76 mm M-36	(Finland/USSR)
	ZSU-57AA	(USSR)
	SA-7 SAM	(USSR)
Anti-tank	95 mm SM58-61 RCL	(Finland)
	SS11 ATGW	(France)
Mortars	120 mm M73	(Finland)
Infantry	Finnish designs	

Bicycle mounted Finnish Jägers.

FRANCE

Strength: 330 000 (270 000 conscripts)
Reserves approximately 400 000. Gendarmerie 80 000
Military service: One year
Background: One of the oldest and most professional armies in Europe, France is not a member of the integrated military command of NATO, though in all other respects she is a full member. The French forces are organised into four main groupings, the Nuclear Strategic Force, the Intervention Force, the Manoeuvre Force and the Territorial Defence Force. The titles are more or less self-explanatory, the Intervention Force being a light mobile formation intended for reinforcement overseas or for operations in support of overseas allies. The Territorial Defence Force is mainly composed of reservists. It acts in very close liaison with the civil administration though national security would be left to the gendarmerie. The Manoeuvre Force consists mainly of the 1st French Army which has troops in West Germany and France, and composes the main striking force of the regular army. Regular recruitment is good and training is thorough. There are many well-equipped schools of instruction and all conscripts devote half of their service time to training. Morale is high, and there is no doubt that the French Army is a significant force in Europe, and its nuclear element makes it a useful counter in the endless super-power arguments.

VAB APC of French Army with 120 mm mortar. (I. V. Hogg)

Structure: The composition of the four Forces would vary according to war needs, although more or less fixed in peacetime. There is one army HQ, three corps and 15 divisions with some independent brigades and regiments in addition. Within the infantry there are different sorts of unit: the metropolitan units which make up most of the armoured divisional infantry strength; the alpine infantry, half of which is mechanised; the Foreign Legion and the overseas units in the colonies. Inside France there are 7 military regions, overseas there are four joint commands—Polynesia, South Indian Ocean, West Indies and Pacific. The reserves in the Territorial Defence Force are organised into 70 infantry battalions and 7 armoured car regiments, forming 27 infantry regiments on mobilisation.

1 army HQ
3 corps HQ
8 armoured divisions
4 infantry divisions
1 parachute division
1 alpine division
1 air-portable division
5 independent SSM regiments
5 SAM regiments

Equipment: The French armaments industry is one of the largest and best-known in the world. It is largely state-financed and the output and quality is considerable. Some weapons are produced in collaboration with foreign firms,

FRANCE

particularly those in West Germany, but in general terms the French Army is entirely equipped with French equipment.

AFVs Tanks	AMX-30 medium	(France)	1000
	AMX-13 light	(France)	1100
Armoured cars	EBR Panhard	(France)	460
	AML 60/90	(France)	450
APCs	AMX-10, AMX-VC1	(France)	500
	AMX-13 VTT	(France)	1500
	VAB	(France)	500
SP guns	155 mm AMX	(France)	180
	155 mm GCT	(France)	
	105 mm AMX	(France)	170
Artillery	155 mm Model 50	(France)	115
	105 mm pack	(France)	200
	Pluton SSM	(France)	
Anti-tank	106 mm M40A1 RCL	(USA)	
	SS11/12 ATGW	(France)	
	MILAN ATGW	(France)	
	HOT ATGW	(France)	
Mortars	120 mm	(France)	260
Infantry	All weapons French in origin		

The Apilas Manurhin shoulder-fired anti-tank missile under development for the French Army. (I. V. Hogg)

GABON

Strength: 1000
Gendarmerie 1600. No formed reserves
Background: Secure in the belief that France will always maintain the sanctity of her frontiers, Gabon is not disposed to use her small GNP for any extensive military force. The army consists of one infantry battalion with a few extra companies and a Presidential Guard. Weapons and equipment are predominantly French.
1 infantry battalion
1 Presidential Guard
2 commando companies
1 engineer and service company
Equipment

AFVs Armoured cars	AML-90	(France)	5
	V-150 Commando	(USA)	6
APCs	VXB	(France)	12
Anti-tank	106 mm RCL	(USA via France)	
Mortars	81 mm	(France)	

GERMANY, DEMOCRATIC REPUBLIC

Strength: 107 000
Reserves, 200 000
Military service: 18 months
Background: The Nationale Volksarmee (NVA) has grown up from an armed police force instituted by the Soviets after the Second World War and the army was in being by the mid-1950s. It has the role of being a symbol of sovereignty of the Republic and a reliable support for the regime. Theoretically it is an independent national force, but in fact it is totally committed to the Warsaw Pact and is under complete Soviet control. One reason for this control is the Soviet fear of a re-armed Germany. The influence of the communist party is strong in the army and it is a most reliable and dedicated force which was allowed to take part in the invasion of Czechoslovakia in 1968.

Structure: The six divisions of the Field Force are stationed in two military districts with other units under control of the Ministry of Defence in Berlin. This gives a heavy concentration in the north and south of the country and around Berlin. All units and formations are precise copies of Soviet Army, but like so many WP armies the divisions tend to be below strength relying on reservists to make them up for war.
2 tank divisions
4 motor rifle divisions
2 SSM brigades
2 artillery regiments
2 AA regiments
1 parachute battalion
2 anti-tank battalions

Equipment: East Germany only makes a few small arms and some ammunition for them. It appears to be deliberate Soviet policy not to allow an arms industry to be built up, hence all war material is imported from the USSR.

AFVs	Tanks	T-54/55	(USSR)	2500 approx
		PT-76 light	(USSR)	120
		T-34 medium (in storage)	(USSR)	600
Scout cars		BRDM 1/2	(USSR)	} 880
		FUG-70	(Hungary)	
APCs		BMP	(USSR)	} 1500
		BTR-40/50/60/152	(USSR)	
SP guns		SU-76	(USSR)	
		SU-100	(USSR)	
		122 mm M-1974	(USSR)	

Artillery	152 mm D-20/M1937	(USSR)	72
	122 mm D-74/M1937/D-30	(USSR)	} 330
	100 mm M1955/T-12	(USSR)	
	85 mm D-44/M52	(USSR)	
	240 mm BM-24 MRS	(USSR)	
	122 mm BM-21/M1972 MRS	(USSR)	100
	100 mm KS-19 AA	(USSR)	100
	57 mm S-60/ZSU-57 AA	(USSR)	100
	23 mm ZU-23/ZSU-23 AA	(USSR)	100
	SA-4 Ganef SAM	(USSR)	
	SA-6 Gainful SAM	(USSR)	
Anti-tank	Sagger ATGW	(USSR)	
Mortars	120 mm M43	(USSR)	250
Infantry	Mixture of imported Soviet equipment and locally-produced variants		

GERMANY, FEDERAL REPUBLIC

Strength: 340 000 (180 000 conscripts)
Reserves, 615 000. Territorial Army 440 000. Border Police 20 000. Internal Security Forces 15 000
Military service: 15 months
Background: The Bundeswehr was formed in January 1955 and in ten years it reached its planned strength of 12 divisions. This army is entirely assigned to NATO and there are carefully designed constitutional checks to ensure that it does not interfere in the running of the country. In contrast, the TA is an entirely national force for home defence, but also acts in support of the active army. The active, or Field, army is divided into three corps which are stationed across the country within the NATO framework. The divisions contain four types of brigade, armoured, armoured infantry, infantry or mountain infantry and airborne. These brigades are grouped into divisions with the same characteristics as the brigades. Conscripts are given three months training in their particular military speciality and then posted to their unit where their more general training has to be completed in the following twelve months. Officer and NCO training is undertaken at special schools and the standards are high. Despite the handicap of a short conscription period and some civilian resistance to the idea of an army at all, the Bundeswehr is a large and competent force well able to take its place alongside any other army in NATO and to make a significant contribution to the Alliance.

Bundeswehr Marder APC. (I. V. Hogg)

Structure: Each corps controls an artillery brigade, an engineer and a signal brigade. Each division has a reconnaissance regiment, an artillery regiment which includes Honest John SAM and an engineer and a signals battalion.
3 corps HQ (including corps troops)
12 divisional HQ (including divisional troops)
16 armoured brigades (each with 2 tank battalions, 1 armoured infantry battalion and 1 armoured artillery battalion)
12 armoured infantry brigades (each with 2 armoured infantry battalions, 1 tank battalion, 1 armoured artillery battalion)
3 light infantry brigades (Jäger) (each with 3 motorised infantry battalions, 1 tank destroyer battalion, 1 artillery battalion)
2 mountain brigades (each with 3 infantry battalions, 1 light artillery battalion)
3 airborne brigades (each with 3 parachute infantry battalions, engineer, anti-tank companies)
15 SSM battalions (with Honest John and Lance)
3 army aviation commands
Equipment: West Germany has a large and comprehensive arms industry which produces most of the weapons and equipment for the army. A proportion of the designs are either licensed from other NATO countries, or are produced in collaboration with them. Many of the heavier artillery pieces and the helicopters are from the USA.

GERMANY, FEDERAL REPUBLIC

AFVs Tanks	Leopard I MBT	(West Germany)	2500
	M48A/5 medium	(USA)	1300
Armoured cars	SPz 2 Luchs	(West Germany)	400
	SPz 11-2 (Hotchkiss)	(France)	1500
APCs	M113	(USA)	4000
	Marder	(FRG)	2000
	HS-30	(Switzerland)	470
SP guns	203 mm M110	(USA)	70
	175 mm M107	(USA)	150
	90 mm Jagdpanzer Kanone	(West Germany)	770
	SS12 Jagdpanzer Rakete	(West Germany)	
	HOT Jagdpanzer Rakete	(West Germany)	
	35 mm × 2 Gepard AA	(West Germany)	200

Artillery	155 mm M114/59	(USA)	56
	155 mm FH-70	(West Germany)	
	105 mm M56 pack	(Italy)	250
	105 mm M101	(USA)	
	Honest John SSM	(USA)	65
	Lance SSM	(USA)	26
	Redeye SAM	(USA)	
	Roland SAM	(France/ West Germany)	
Anti-tank	106 mm RCL	(USA)	200
	TOW ATGW	(USA)	350
	MILAN ATGW	(France/ West Germany) (more on order)	850
	HOT ATGW	(France/ West Germany)	
Mortars	120 mm MRS-120-2	(Israel)	956
Infantry	9 mm UZI SMG	(Israel)	

All other infantry weapons are West German designs

German paratrooper-weapons are G3 rifle and PZF 44 RCL.
(C. Foss)

GHANA

Strength: 15 000
Reserves, 1000. Border Guard 3000
Military service: Voluntary
Background: Ghana gained independence in 1957 and from then until 1966 the country was ruled by President Nkrumah. He was overthrown in a military and police coup and for three years the army jointly ruled. There was another military coup in 1972 and since then there have been a few examples of unrest among some officers. The army is nevertheless an efficient force well capable of defending the country's frontiers and supplying contingents to UN peacekeeping multi-national forces.
Structure: The army consists of two infantry brigades with a few independent units and a single parachute battalion. Battalions tend to be posted singly around the country. The Border Guard is organised into three battalions and is mainly based in the Eastern Region.
2 infantry brigade HQ
6 infantry battalions
1 reconnaissance battalion
1 mortar battalion
1 field engineer battalion
1 signals company
1 airborne battalion (under strength)
Equipment: There is no indigenous arms industry, and most of the equipment is imported from Britain though there was a short period when Soviet weapons were in use.

AFVs Armoured cars	Ferret	(UK)	26
	Saladin	(UK)	10
	MOWAG	(Switzerland)	65
Artillery	105 mm M-56 pack	(Italy)	
	76 mm M1942	(USSR)	
Anti-tank	84 mm Carl Gustaf RCL	(Sweden)	
Mortars	120 mm M-65	(Israel)	10

Ghanaian troops serving with UNIFIL forces in Southern Lebanon. (Ghanaian MOD/MARS)

GREECE

Strength: 145 000 (123 000 conscripts)
Reserves, approximately 250 000. National Guard 70 000. Gendarmerie 30 000
Military service: 30 months
Background: Greece was ruled by a corrupt and inefficient military junta from 1967 to 1974. The last act of the junta was to precipitate the war with Turkey on Cyprus and the Greeks were humiliated. Since then the army has been steadily built up at some cost to the country in terms of foreign expenditure. The role of the army is twofold, firstly to defend the north of the country against Soviet attack and secondly to counter Turkey. The majority of the army is deployed in the north, though there is now a trend towards the Turkish side of the country. Military liability extends from the age of 21 to 50. After his conscription service a man will pass into the First Reserve for 19 years and 10 years in the Second Reserve. Women can be called up for 14 months service if required.

Structure: The Greek Army is primarily an infantry force and the proportion of armour is low. There are some independent commando-type formations and a small number of SAM units. The tactics and training of all are predominantly American in origin.

- 1 armoured division
- 11 infantry divisions
- 2 independent armoured brigades
- 1 para-commando brigade
- 1 marine infantry brigade
- 2 SSM battalions
- 1 SAM battalion
- 12 artillery battalions
- 14 army aviation companies

Euromissile MILAN ATGW now entering service with the Greek Army. (C. Foss)

GREECE

Equipment: The Greek arms industry is small, but increasing. However, for the present all except small arms have to be imported.

AFVs	Tanks			
		M47 medium	(USA)	150
		M48 medium	(USA)	800
		AMX-30 medium	(France)	170
		M24 light	(USA)	190
APCs		M113	(USA)	520
		AMX-10P	(France)	
		M59	(USA)	460
		MOWAG	(Switzerland)	
SP guns		203 mm M110	(USA)	
		175 mm M107	(USA)	
		155 mm M44/109	(USA)	
		105 mm M52	(USA)	

Artillery	203 mm M115	(USA)	
	155 mm M59/114	(USA)	240
	105 mm M101	(USA)	80
	75 mm M116 pack	(USA)	100
	Honest John SSM	(USA)	
	90 mm M116 AA	(USA)	
	75 mm M51 AA	(USA)	
	40 mm M1 AA	(Sweden)	
	20 mm twin Rh 202 AA	(West Germany)	
	Hawk SAM	(USA)	
Anti-tank	106 mm M40A1 RCL	(USA)	
	SS11 ATGW	(France)	
	Cobra ATGW	(West Germany)	
	MILAN ATGW	(France)	
Infantry	Predominantly US in origin but some West German designs now being introduced		

GUATEMALA

Strength: 15 000
Reserves, approximately 3000
Military service: Two years
Background: Guatemala has been beset by guerrilla war inside the country since the 1960s and the army has virtually taken over the country in all but name. There has been a formal state of siege since 1971. It is difficult to assess the fighting ability of the army since it is widely spread throughout the country for reasons of internal security. At the same time, the army conducts an effective education programme among the villages. Reservists are also meant to receive training, but probably do not. The recall of reservists is not practised.
Structure: The Army consists of 10 infantry battalions and three brigade headquarters, together with the Presidential Guard and other independent units. It is likely that the brigades are never formed or exercised and the largest operational formation would be the battalion.

 3 brigade HQ
10 infantry battalions
 1 Presidential Guard battalion
 1 artillery battery
 1 armoured company
 1 engineer battalion
 1 parachute battalion (unlikely to be fully trained)

Equipment: Guatemala has no arms industry and all equipment is imported. Relations with the USA have fluctuated recently and arms are being bought from Europe and Israel, though the bulk of all equipment is elderly US purchases.

AFVs	Tanks	M4 medium	(USA)	10
		M3A1 light	(USA)	10
	APCs	M3A1	(USA)	6
		M113	(USA)	10
		RBY-1	(Israel)	10
		Cadillac-Gage Commando	(USA)	7
Artillery		105 mm M101	(USA)	12
		75 mm M116	(USA)	12
Mortars		4.2 in M30	(USA)	
		81 mm M29	(USA)	
Infantry		Largely US in origin		

GUNIEA

Strength: Between 5000 and 8000
Para-military forces, 8000
Military service: Voluntary
Background: Guinea is an ex-French colony which unusually has broken all links with France. Despite this the army retains a strong French flavour, though it is largely equipped and trained by the USSR and perhaps Cuba. It is likely that the effectiveness of the units is low and information on precise strengths and states of training is difficult to obtain.
Structure: There appears to be no operational formation.
1 armoured battalion
4 infantry battalions
1 engineer battalion
Equipment: Most of the weapons and equipment in Guinea have come from the USSR or China, with smaller quantities from Czechoslovakia. Maintenance is no doubt very poor.

AFVs Tanks	T-34 medium	(USSR)	25-30
	PT-76 light	(USSR)	10
APCs	BTR-40/152	(USSR)	30-40
Artillery	122 mm M1931	(USSR)	
	85 mm D-44	(USSR)	
	76 mm M1942	(USSR)	

GUYANA

Strength: 2000
Military service: Voluntary
Background: The army is both new and small. Its role is to safeguard the frontiers against two neighbours in particular, Venezuela and Surinam, both of whom have laid claim to some of Guyana's territory. However, a more likely use for the army would be as an internal security force.
Structure: 2 infantry battalions
Equipment: All equipment is British.

AFVs Armoured cars	Shorland	(UK)	4
Mortars	81 mm	(UK)	12

HAITI

Strength: 6000
Para-military forces, 15 000
Military service: Voluntary
Background: For more than 100 years the role of the Haitian army has been internal security and now only three units could undertake any sort of conventional military operation. The army is spread around the country in small sub-units and acts as an armed police force, entirely subservient to the government. Military service is an honoured profession and recruitment is generally for life.
Structure: The main strength lies in 35 or more infantry companies spread around the country. The formed battalions are kept in or close to the capital.
1 infantry battalion
Presidential Guard (battalion size)
1 'commando' battalion
20-30 infantry companies
Equipment: Most of the equipment is somewhat elderly and of US origin.

AFVs	APCs	M113	(USA)
		V-150 Commando	(USA)
Artillery		105 mm M1	(USA)
		75 mm M116 pack	(USA)
Infantry		US origin	

HONDURAS

Strength: 10-12 000
Para-military forces, 3000
Military service: Voluntary, made up with conscripts for 8 months term of service
Background: After the war with El Salvador in 1969 the army was reorganised and improved. Internal security problems during the 1970s have probably not helped training or morale and the army is not a particularly effective force for conventional operations, however it is better than it has been for many years.
Structure: The largest operational formation is a battalion and there is no experience of handling any sort of battle formation. Most of the units are spread throughout the country's six administrative districts.
10 infantry battalions
1 Presidential Guard unit
2 artillery battalions
1 engineer battalion
1 signals battalion
Equipment: Nearly all the army equipment is US in origin, though the army now carries FN rifles and the air force is buying Israeli aircraft.

AFVs	Tanks	Scorpion light	(UK)	on order
Artillery		105 mm M101	(USA)	12
		75 mm M116 pack	(USA)	12
Mortars		120 mm	(perhaps Israeli)	

HUNGARY

Strength: 80 000 (50 000 conscripts)
Reserves, 160 000. Border Guards, 15 000. Workers Militia 60 000
Military service: Two years
Background: Hungary is a people's republic and the constitution states that military service and the defence of the country are the duties of all citizens. It is this idea which has brought about the large Workers Militia units in the factories and towns. The role of the army is a dual one of maintaining internal security and defending the country against external aggression. However, it is most unlikely that Hungary would be allowed to make any military actions on her own. All operations would be part of a Warsaw Pact combined plan. It seems unlikely that the standard of unit training can be very high and it is uncertain how often the army formations are actually exercised in the field.

Structure: The organisation of the army closely follows the Soviet pattern, one of the five motor rifle divisions is thought to be at cadre strength only. The tank divisions are stationed in west Hungary, the motor rifle divisions in the centre. The Soviet Southern Group of Forces is also in Hungary, with its HQ in Budapest. This is four divisions strong, and obviously presents a firm reminder of the Soviet hold over its satellites.

1 tank division (probably another in cadre)
5 motor rifle divisions (another in cadre)
1 SSM brigade (Scud)
3 artillery regiments
2 AA battalions
1 airborne battalion

FUG-63 amphibious scout car of the Hungarian Army.

HUNGARY

Equipment: A few items are produced in Hungary, based on the Soviet pattern, but the main inventory of military equipment is Soviet, and bought from the Soviet Union directly.

AFVs Tanks	T-34/54/55 medium	(USSR)	1000
	PT-76 light	(USSR)	100
Scout cars	BRDM	(USSR)	600
	FUG-63	(Hungary)	
APCs	BTR-40/50/60/152	(USSR)	1500
Artillery	152 mm D-1/D-20/M1937	(USSR)	80
	130 mm M-46	(USSR)	
	122 mm D-30/D-74/ M1937/M1938	(USSR)	250
	100 mm M1955	(USSR)	
	85 mm D-44	(USSR)	
	122 mm BM-21 RL	(USSR)	40
	Frog SSM	(USSR)	24
	Scud SSM	(USSR)	12
	ZSU-23-4 AA	(USSR)	50
	ZSU-57-2 AA	(USSR)	50
	SA-6 Gainful SAM	(USSR)	20
	SA-7 SAM	(USSR)	300
	SA-9 Gaskin SAM	(USSR)	50
Anti-tank	57 mm M1942	(USSR)	200
	Sagger ATGW	(USSR)	100
	Snapper ATGW	(USSR)	
Mortars	120 mm M43	(USSR)	100
	82 mm M37	(USSR)	300
Infantry	Entirely Soviet in origin		

INDIA

Strength: 950 000
Reserves, 200 000. Territorial Army, 40 000
Military service: Voluntary
Background: The Indian Army has retained much of its original British character, though it went through a bad patch during the first two decades of independence. Since 1970 there has been a marked improvement and it now once again ranks as one of the best-trained and least politically-involved armies in South Asia. It has managed to retain its historic role as a highly trained instrument for the defence of the country and has left internal security to the police. Army service is highly respected and recruiting is by selection from the many applicants. Long service is normal and as a consequence units and formations are competent and capable. There have been six actual wars in which the Indian army has fought since 1947 and in addition units are provided for the UN peacekeeping forces.

Structure: At unit level the army is strongly regimental, an inheritance from the British which has not been allowed to lapse, and operational formations are also British. There is an emphasis on mountain troops, a reflection of the nature of the northern and eastern frontiers.

  2 armoured divisions
 16 infantry divisions
 11 mountain divisions
  5 independent armoured brigades
  1 independent infantry brigade
  1 parachute brigade
 14 independent artillery brigades (approximately 20 AA regiments, 4 artillery observation squadrons, some independent flights)

Indian troops displaying WW2 vintage British equipment and Indian manufactured FN rifles. (I. V. Hogg)

INDIA

Equipment: There is a long history of arms manufacture in India and there are now about 20 factories producing all manner of military equipment from aircraft downwards. The country now produces small arms, artillery, ammunition, assembles B vehicles, makes a tank under licence and makes some ATGW under licence. However, the army is equipped with a mixture of weapons dating from the 1960s when it was imperative to stock up quickly.

AFVs	Tanks	Centurion Mk 5/7	(UK)	50
		T-54/55 medium	(USSR)	900
		Vijayanta medium	(India)	900
		PT-76 light	(USSR)	50
		AMX-13 light	(France)	
	APCs	BTR-50/152	(USSR)	700
		OT-62/64	(Czechoslovakia)	
	SP guns	105 mm Abbott	(UK)	

Artillery	203 mm M115	(USA)	550
	155 mm M114	(USA)	
	5.5 in	(UK)	
	130 mm M46	(USSR)	
	105 mm M101	(USA)	300
	100 mm M1944/ M1955	(USSR)	
	76 mm M-48	(USSR)	2000 approx
	25 pdr	(UK)	
	75 mm M116 pack	(USA)	
	40 mm L/70 AA	(Sweden)	
	ZSU-23-4 AA	(USSR)	
	Tigercat SAM	(UK)	40
	SA-6 Gainful SAM	(USSR)	
Anti-tank	57 mm M43	(USSR)	
	ENTAC ATGW	(France)	
Mortars	160 mm M1943	(USSR)	500
	120 mm M37	(USSR)	
Infantry	Mixture of British and USSR weapons		

INDONESIA

Strength: 180 000
Reserves, 35 000. Police Mobile Brigade, 12 000. Militia, 100 000
Military service: Voluntary, with limited selective service for some specialists
Background: Since independence in 1949 the Indonesian Army has been integrated into the population and at any one time at least one third of the military strength is engaged in civil and administrative duties. In fact, the Army largely helps to run the country. Units are deployed in four main regions containing no less than 17 military commands. Although officer and NCO training is of a high standard and competition for places in the various colleges is severe, the general level of operation in the army is not good. There are few realistic exercises and maintenance is poor. There is little money to spare for training ammunition and the artillery, in particular, practise too rarely. Recruiting is good, and the only conscripts are such specialists as doctors.

Structure: It seems unlikely that there is any formation above brigade, and that operates more as an administrative HQ than an operational grouping. It is likely that the majority of the army cannot function effectively at a higher level than that of the unit.

- 1 armoured brigade (light units, in strategic reserve)
- 14 infantry brigades (each with approximately 5 infantry battalions, 1 artillery battalion, 1 AA battalion. 10 engineer battalions spread among where needed)
- 2 airborne infantry battalions (insufficient aircraft to fly more than about 1 company)
- 5 field artillery regiments
- 4 AA regiments

Indonesia has recently taken delivery of French AMX-10 PAC 90 fire support vehicle. (C. Foss)

INDONESIA

Equipment: There is a local arms industry which makes small arms and ammunition. All larger equipments are imported. The army has a mixture of Soviet, British and French, much of which is out of service.

AFVs Tanks	M3A1 medium	(USA)	100
	AMX-13 light	(France)	150
	PT-76 light	(USSR)	75
Armoured cars	Saladin	(UK)	75
	Ferret	(UK)	55
APCs	AMX-VCI	(France)	
	Saracen	(UK)	
	V-150 Commando	(USA)	60
	BTR-40/60/152	(USSR)	130

Artillery	122 mm M1938	(USSR)	
	105 mm M56, M101	(USA)	40
	76 mm M48	(USSR)	50
	57 mm S-60 AA	(USSR)	
	40 mm AA	(USA-Sweden)	200
Anti-tank	106 mm M40A1 RCL	(USA)	
	ENTAC ATGW	(France)	
Mortars	120 mm M43	(USSR)	200
	81 mm M1937	(USSR)	
Infantry	Mixture of Soviet, French and local licenced manufacture		

IRAN

Strength: 285 000
Reserves, 300 000. Para-military (Gendarmerie, Police), 70,000
Military service: One year
Background: Any information on the Iranian armed forces has to be heavily qualified and taken as being at best approximate. The revolution since the fall of the Shah together with the war with Iraq makes it extremely difficult to estimate with any accuracy what has happened to the Army, and what is currently happening. The Iraqi war has at least shown that the Iranian Army has not entirely disintegrated in the internal turmoil of the country, but it has shown that it lacks much in command, control and equipment maintenance. How long it will take to return to its former condition, if it ever does, is pure speculation.

Structure: Under the Shah there were three Field Armies and an Imperial Guard. The following list is based on this structure but now needs to be heavily modified.
3 armoured divisions
3 infantry divisions
1 independent armoured brigade
1 independent infantry brigade
1 independent airborne brigade
1 independent special forces brigade
4 independent SAM battalions

IRAN

Equipment: It is likely that practically all of the army equipment remains in Iran, less any war losses, but its state of maintenance must be poor. There have been no supplies of spares for over a year, nor any skilled western advice.

AFVs Tanks	Chieftain	(UK)	875
	M48	(USA)	400
	M60A1	(USA)	460
Reconnaissance vehicles	Scorpion	(UK)	250
APCs	M113	(USA)	320
	BMP	(USSR)	
	BTR-40/50/60/152	(USSR)	500
SP guns	203 mm M110	(USA)	14
	175 mm M107	(USA)	38
	155 mm M109	(USA)	440

Artillery	203 mm M115	(USA)	14
	155 mm M114	(USA)	112
	130 mm M46	(USSR)	
	105 mm M101	(USA)	330
	75 mm M116 pack	(USA)	
	122 mm BM-21 RL	(USSR)	72
	23 mm, 35 mm, 40 mm, 57 mm, 85 mm AA		1,800
	23 mm ZSU-23-4/ 57-2 AA	(USSR)	100
	Hawk SAM	(USA)	
Anti-tank	106 mm M40A1 RCL	(USA)	
	ENTAC, SS11, SS12 ATGW	(France)	
	TOW, Dragon ATGW	(USA)	
Infantry	Mostly US in origin, but with certain items from West Germany and Israel		

The Israeli UZI 9 mm SMG as used by Iran. (C. Foss)

IRAQ

Strength: 190 000
Reserves, 260 000
Military service: Two years
Background: The Iraqi Army is in a difficult position since it has three main roles to fulfil. The first is that it protects the government and maintains it in power. For this there is a large garrison in Baghdad and a general reserve at Tikrit. It is unlikely that either of these would be used to reinforce an action elsewhere, and it appears that in the present war with Iran these troops have largely stayed in place. The second role is to maintain internal security, not an easy task in a country with deep religious divisions, and the third is to safeguard the frontiers. In the present war with Iran it is apparent that much has gone wrong, and due to the need to keep strong forces inside the country the full strength of the army cannot be deployed. It is interesting to note that despite the reasonable reputation that the Iraqis have always had among Middle Eastern armies, their performance in the Iranian war has been poor and lacking in determined leadership.

Structure: For the last two decades the deployment of the army has been to station roughly half in the northern part of the country; this will now be sharply reduced in numbers due to the war. Operationally it does not seem as if the army had a higher headquarters than division, which may partly explain the reverses in Iran.
4 armoured divisions
2 mechanised divisions
4 infantry divisions
1 mechanised brigade (Republican Guard)
2 independent infantry brigades
1 special forces brigade

Iraq uses the Brazilian ENGESA EE-11 Urutu 6 × 6 APC.

Equipment: The majority of the equipment is Soviet in origin, though there has been some buying from France. An indeterminate number of Soviet technicians assist in the maintenance of this equipment and in general it has always been assumed that the standards of readiness were high. The war with Iran has not so far disclosed any startling equipment deficiencies.

AFVs Tanks	T-54/55/62	(USSR)	1700
	T-34	(USSR)	100
	PT-76 light	(USSR)	100
APCs	BMP	(USSR)	200
	BTR-50/60/152	(USSR)	
	OT-62	(Czechoslovakia)	
	VCR	(France)	
	EE-11	(Brazil)	
SP guns	122 mm SU-122	(USSR)	40
	100 mm SU-100	(USSR)	90

Artillery	152 mm M1937	(USSR)	
	130 mm M46	(USSR)	
	122 mm M1937/8	(USSR)	800
	85 mm D-44	(USSR)	
	75 mm	(USA)	
	Scud B SSM	(USSR)	
	Frog-7 SSM	(USSR)	

	100 mm		
	85 mm		
	57 mm		
	37 mm	AA (USSR)	1200
	23 mm		
	ZSU-23-4		
	ZSU-57-2		

Anti-tank	Sagger ATGW	(USSR)
	SS11 ATGW	(France)
	MILAN ATGW	(France)
Mortars	120 mm/160 mm	(USSR)
Infantry	Entirely Soviet in origin	

IRELAND

Strength: 13 500
Reserves, 18 600
Military service: Voluntary
Background: The official description of the army is that it is essentially defensive in its primary mission and the structure and equipment of the units make it unlikely that it could do more than offer limited resistance to any incursion. It is, however, also maintained as the ultimate guarantee of law and order within the State. Contingents are regularly sent to the various UN peacekeeping forces. Standards of training are good at all levels.
Structure: The largest operational formation is the brigade, and the army is predominantly an infantry force. Many units in these brigades are actually reserve status and are probably below strength.
6 infantry brigades (10 battalions)
1 independent infantry battalion
Independent artillery batteries, field engineer companies and AA batteries

Equipment: Ireland has no traditional arms industry, but some items are being manufactured now. However, most weapons and equipment are imported from UK, or more recently, France and Sweden.

AFVs			
Reconnaissance vehicles	Scorpion	(UK)	on order
Armoured cars	AML 60/90	(France)	42
	Panhard VTT M3	(France)	50
	Unimog	(Switzerland)	10
	Timoney	(Ireland)	10
Artillery	25 pdr	(UK)	48
	105 mm Light Gun	(UK)	
	40 mm Bofors AA	(Sweden)	26
Anti-tank	90 mm PV-1110 RCL	(Sweden)	60
	MILAN ATGW	(France)	on order
Mortars	120 mm Tampella	(Finland)	72
	81 mm	(Sweden)	200
Infantry	FAL rifles	(Belgium)	
	MAG:MG	(Belgium)	

ISRAEL

Strength: 138 000 (120 000 conscripts). On mobilisation, 375 000
Reserves, 450 000 for all arms
Military service: Three years (Women two years)
Background: Israel is almost the only example of a nation in arms since the published figures (which are difficult to obtain and impossible to verify) do not show the ultimate mobilisation ability of the country. All able-bodied citizens have a war task and all vehicles and semi-military equipment are listed for mobilisation. For too long has Israel lived under the daily threat of invasion for any citizen to be in the least complacent or unprepared. The army has a fairly small regular core and relies on a rapid build-up in emergencies. The country is sufficiently small and well-motivated to be able to use this system. The mobilisation figure of about 400 000 is achieved within 24 hours, every man and woman being fully trained and knowing exactly what to do. Reservists have a commitment to the age of 54 and the state of training of all is extremely high. Leaders are young at all levels and the principle is to lead from the front. The army is remarkably efficient and capable as its performance in the several wars since 1948 clearly shows.

Structure: The organisation of the army is highly centralised and the most usual operational formation is the brigade. In the Yom Kippur War it does seem that a loose divisional organisation was used, but this is not apparently a normal practice. About 11 brigades are kept at full strength and a further 6 at half strength. All others exist at cadre level only.

24 armoured brigades (5 at full strength, 1 at 50%)
 9 mechanised brigades (4 at half strength)
 9 infantry brigades (4 at full strength)
 5 parachute brigades (2 at full strength, 1 at 50%)
 9 artillery brigades

US supplied tracked Chaparral anti-aircraft system of the Israeli Army. (C. Foss)

ISRAEL

Equipment: The general policy for equipment in Israel seems to be to achieve independence of all imports by local manufacture. This is accompanied by a vigorous export drive, but present stocks are very mixed and the remaining quantities of battle-worthy Sherman tanks has become legendary. Israel has bought arms where she could and these have been topped up by war booty, all of which is utilised. The resulting mixture must be an ordnance officer's nightmare.

AFVs			
Tanks	Centurion	(UK)	1000
	M48	(USA)	650
	M60	(USA)	800
	M4 Sherman	(USA)	
	T-54/55	(USSR)	400
	PT-76	(USSR)	65
	Merkava	(Israel)	40
Armoured cars	AML-60/90	(France)	
	RBY Ramata	(Israel)	
	BRDM	(USSR)	
APCs	M113	(USA)	
	BTR-40/50/60/152	(USSR)	
SP guns	203 mm M110	(USA)	48
	175 mm M107	(USA)	60
	155 mm Sherman	(Israel)	120
	155 mm M109	(USA)	
	105 mm M7	(USA)	

Artillery		
155 mm M114	(USA)	⎫
130 mm M46	(USSR)	⎬ 450
122 mm D-30	(USSR)	⎭
105 mm M101	(USA)	500
240 mm BM-24 RL	(USSR)	
122 mm BM-21 RL	(USSR)	
Lance SSM	(USA)	
20/40 mm AA	(various)	
Hawk SAM	(USA)	
Chaparral SAM	(USA)	
Redeye SAM	(USA)	

Anti-tank		
106 mm M40A1 RCL	(USA)	
Sagger ATGW	(USA)	
TOW ATGW	(USA)	
Dragon ATGW	(USA)	
Cobra ATGW	(West Germany)	
SS11 ATGW	(France)	

Mortars		
160 mm Soltam	(Israel)	
120 mm Soltam	(Israel)	

Infantry		
Galil rifle	(Israel)	
FAL rifle	(Belgium)	
MAG MG	(Belgium)	

ITALY

Strength: 250 000 (160 000 conscripts)
Reserves approximately 550 000
Military service: One year
Background: The role of the Italian Army, as defined by its own Foreign Ministry, is the defence of the north-eastern frontier and the internal defence of the country. In this latter task the main responsibility is taken by the Carabinieri, and so far the army has not had to be called in. The entire army is consigned to NATO and one Alpini battalion and an artillery unit are assigned to the ACE Mobile Force. There are no Italian troops outside Italy and none in the UN peacekeeping forces. Conscripts are given three months basic training followed by four months specialist training, which leaves very little time for unit service. As a result most of the operational units are regular. After conscript service all men have a commitment to the reserve until aged 45.

Structure: The Army is divided into the Field Army and the Territorial Army. The latter undertakes responsibility for recruiting, mobilisation and internal security. The Field Army is made by three corps of seven divisions and some independent brigades.
3 corps HQ
2 armoured divisions
5 infantry divisions (partially mechanised)
1 independent mechanised brigade
5 alpine brigades
1 airborne brigade
1 marine brigade
1 missile brigade

Equipment: Italy has a large and active arms industry which makes practically every class of weapon and vehicle. The West German Leopard tank is made under licence and so are other armoured vehicles. Although the artillery has many US guns, OTO Melara is well able to make them and the 105 mm pack howitzer has been a most successful export project; also the country is a partner in the FH and SP 70 guns. The Italian electronics industry can hold its own with the rest of the world, and there is a flourishing export trade in ammunition and fuses.

AFVs	Tanks	Leopard	(West Germany)	654
		M60	(USA)	200
		M47 light	(USA)	700
APCs		M106	(USA)	
		M113	(USA)	4000
		M548	(USA)	
		M577	(USA)	
SP guns		203 mm M110	(USA)	24
		175 mm M107	(USA)	36
		155 mm M109	(USA)	200
		155 mm M44	(USA)	100

Artillery	203 mm M115	(USA)	
	155 mm M59	(USA)	
	155 mm FH 70	(International)	1500
	105 mm M101	(USA)	
	105 mm M-56 pack	(Italy)	335
	Lance SSM	(USA)	6
	40 mm AA	(Sweden)	
	Hawk SAM	(USA)	
Anti-tank	106 mm RCL	(USA)	
	57 mm RCL	(USA)	
	Cobra ATGW	(West Germany)	
	SS11 ATGW	(France)	
	TOW ATGW	(USA)	
Mortars	120 mm	(France)	
	107 mm	(USA)	
Infantry	Almost all weapons of Italian manufacture		

Italian paratroops with air-dropped 105 mm pack howitzer.
(C. Foss)

IVORY COAST

Strength: 4500
Para-military forces, Gendarmerie 3000+
Military service: Voluntary
Background: An ex-French colony, the Ivory Coast has been peaceful since it gained independence. The general tendency of the country is towards France and things French, and this is reflected in the army.
Structure: There is no real structure of the small army, the few units being controlled directly by the government.
3 infantry battalions
1 engineer battalion
1 armoured squadron
1 parachute company
2 artillery batteries
Equipment: Practically every item of army equipment is French.

AFVs Tanks	AMX-13 light	(France)	5
	Armoured cars AML-60/90	(France)	16
Artillery	105 mm howitzers	(France)	4
Mortars	120 mm	(France)	
	81 mm	(France)	

JAMAICA

Strength: 1000
One reserve battalion
Military service: Voluntary
Structure: The very small army of Jamaica is only really suitable as an armed back-up for the police should internal affairs get out of hand.
1 infantry battalion and some supporting units
1 reserve infantry battalion
Equipment: Light weapons only. Largely British in origin.

JAPAN

Strength: 155 000
Reserves, 40 000
Military service: Voluntary
Background: Since 1945 there has been a strong anti-military attitude in the majority of the country and the Self-Defence Force was not set up until 1954. The Basic Policy for the forces states that they exist to forestall aggression and to defend the peace and independence of the country. Troops can be used to assist the police, but it is most unlikely to happen, nor can they be sent outside the country; hence there is no assistance to the UN peacekeeping forces. Training is thorough and largely based on US practice. Since its formation the SDF has had no operational experience at all, but it does assist in emergency work in the civil community and in land work to help farmers.

Structure: The operational formation appears to be the division, which is grouped under an army command. The divisions are smaller than is generally the case in western armies and there are independent units and brigades of artillery and support troops which are allocated to them as required. Formations are deployed with the weight of the defence opposite the Soviet Far Eastern provinces.
  1 mechanised division
12 infantry divisions (two types, A and B. A is stronger)
  1 tank brigade
  1 airborne brigade
  1 composite brigade
  1 artillery brigade
  2 AA brigades
  1 signals brigade
  5 engineer brigades
  8 SAM gps
35 army aircraft squadrons

JAPAN

Equipment: There is a flourishing defence industry in Japan, though it is much hampered by export restrictions. Japan is one of the eleven tank-producing countries.

AFVs Tanks	Type 61	(Japan)	540	
	Type 74	(Japan)	150	
	M41 light	(USA)	70	
APCs	Type 73	(Japan)	} 780	
	Type 60	(Japan)		
SP guns	155 mm M44	(USA)		
	155 mm Type 75	(Japan)	} 75	
	105 mm M52	(USA)		
	105 mm Type 74	(Japan)		
Artillery	203 mm M115	(USA)		
	155 mm M114	(USA)	} 800	
	105 mm M101	(USA)		
	75 mm M116 pack	(USA)		
	30 mm, 40 mm, 57 mm AA	(various)		
	Hawk SAM	(USA)		
Anti-tank	57 mm, 75 mm, 106 mm RCL	(USA)		
	KAM-9 ATGW	(Japan)		
	Type 64 ATGW	(Japan)		
Mortars	107 mm	(USA)	} 1700	
	81 mm	(USA)		
Infantry	Mostly of Japanese manufacture			

106 mm RCL ATG mounting on jeep of Japanese Army.

JIBUTI

Strength: 3600
Military service: Voluntary
Background: The Jibuti Army is really an armed gendarmerie whose main task is the policing of the region. It cannot be assumed that it could make more than a token effort in the event of war.
Structure
2 infantry battalions
1 mixed battalion
1 artillery battalion (under-strength)
Equipment: Practically all military equipment has been supplied by France.

AFVs Tanks	AMX-13 light	(France)
Armoured cars	AML	(France)
Artillery	105 mm guns	(France)

JORDAN

Strength: 60 000
7000 Civil Militia. 3000 Mobile Police. These are the only formed reserves
Military service: Voluntary
Background: The Army is a well-led and highly professional force with a good reputation in the Middle East. It has established itself as an effective army in the various wars with Israel, but its main role is more defensive in character and it is unlikely that it could maintain an offensive outside the country. Training is very good and training missions have often travelled to other neighbouring countries, the entire army is kept at a high state of readiness and is well equipped. Due to the unstable political nature of some of the population the army is used on occasions to maintain internal security and safeguard government. Command is centralised and the largest operational formation is the division. These are smaller than western divisions since they do not have the large administrative 'tail' which is so common in other armies.

Structure: The divisions are triangular in concept with three brigades and three battalions in each. Most of the logistic functions are carried out by static base organisations, which is perfectly practical in a country with such short interior lines. AA units and special forces groups are outside the divisional structure.
2 armoured divisions
2 mechanised division
3 special forces battalions
2 AA brigades

M110 203 mm self-propelled howitzer of Royal Jordanian Army. (Royal Jordanian Army/MARS)

JORDAN

Equipment: There is at present no arms industry of any size in Jordan. Most of the equipment is US in origin with the remainder from the UK. Much of the equipment is quite sophisticated and it is used and maintained to a high standard by well-trained operators and technicians.

AFVs	Tanks	Centurion	(UK)	200
		M47/48/60	(USA)	300
APCs		M113	(USA)	750
		Saracen	(UK)	120
Scout cars		Ferret	(UK)	140
SP guns		155 mm M44	(USA)	20
		105 mm M52	(USA)	35

Artillery	203 mm M110	(USA)	4
	155 mm M59	(USA)	10
	105 mm M101	(USA)	90
	25 pdr	(UK)	110
	40 mm AA	(USA)	
	20 mm Vulcan AA	(USA)	
	Hawk SAM	(USA)	
	Redeye SAM	(USA)	
Anti-tank	106 mm M40A1 RCL	(USA)	
	TOW ATGW	(USA)	
	Dragon ATGW	(USA)	
Mortars	120 mm		
	107 mm	(USA)	
	81 mm	(UK)	
Infantry	Mixture of US, British and West German equipment		

KAMPUCHEA

The present position in Kampuchea is so confused and uncertain that it is not profitable to try and make firm statements. What remains of the once large army is now a guerrilla force in the jungle operating against the Vietnamese who control the major portion of the country. Armament is restricted to light infantry weapons, mostly of US or Chinese origin.

KENYA

Strength: 8000
Para-military forces, 2000 police. There appear to be no formed reserves
Military service: Voluntary
Background: Kenya inherited part of the British East African Army and the infantry battalions now in being were for the most part once King's African Rifles. The country has a formidable problem in guarding its frontiers since the neighbouring states all seem to make some sort of claim to parts of Kenya. At the same time there is a constant threat of internal troubles. Hence the small army is kept very alert, and the state of training is excellent. There is considerable liaison with the UK and the army is very much based on British lines.
Structure: The eventual aim is to have two brigades of three battalions each, but it is taking time to reach this goal and so far the five battalions (one still forming) are operated as independent units.
5 infantry battalions (one forming)
1 engineer battalion
1 support group
1 artillery battalion

Equipment: There is no arms industry and the majority of equipment is British in origin. However, there have been some purchases of French and West German vehicles.

AFVs Tanks	Vickers Mk 3 (UK)	
Armoured cars	AML-60/90 (France)	30
	Saladin (UK)	3
APCs	UR-416 (West Germany)	15
	Panhard M3 (France)	10
Artillery	105 mm	
	light gun (UK)	8

Anti-tank	120 mm	
	Wombat RCL(UK)	
	84 mm Carl	
	Gustaf RCL(UK/Sweden)	56
Mortars	120 mm	
	Soltam (Israel)	8
	81 mm L16 (UK)	20
Infantry	FAL rifle (Belgium)	
	G3 rifle (West Germany)	
	MAG MG (Belgium)	

Vickers Mk 3 MBT of the Kenyan Army. (C. Foss)

KOREA, DEMOCRATIC PEOPLE'S REPUBLIC

Strength: 560 000
Reserves, 1 000 000 (estimated)
Military service: Five years
Background: The declared aim of the army is the defence of the frontier with the South and there is no doubt that the frontier represents the major activity of all units. There is steady pressure against the South, and minor infiltration. In general terms the army resembles that of the Soviet Union and the training and equipment are all but identical. Precise information is hard to come by.

Structure: The army is divided into five 'armies' or 'army groups', each with four or so divisions in it. Each division is organised on the lines of the older-syle Soviet divisions and these divisions are the operational army. The Security Corps is organised into regiments and companies and maintains internal security. Each village and factory has a workers' militia which would form the trained reserve in time of war.

  2 tank divisions
  3 motorised infantry divisions
35 infantry divisions
  4 independent infantry brigades
  3 reconnaissance brigades
  8 independent light infantry brigades
  3 AA divisions
  5 independent tank regiments
  5 airborne battalions
  3 SSM battalions
20 artillery regiments
10 AA regiments

Equipment: There is virtually no indigenous arms industry and the forces have a mixture of weapons, some Soviet, some Chinese and a few left over from the Korean War.

AFVs	Tanks	T-34	(USSR)	350
		T-54/55	(USSR)	1800
		Type 59	(PRC)	
		T-62	(USSR)	52
		PT-76	(USSR)	100
APCs		BTR-40/60/152	(USSR)	
		BMP	(USSR)	

Artillery	152 mm M1937	(USSR)	
	130 mm M46	(USSR)	
	122 mm M1931/38	(USSR)	
	100 mm M1944/55	(USSR)	1800
	85 mm D-44	(USSR)	
	76 mm M1942	(USSR)	
	240 mm BM-24 RL	(USSR)	
	200 mm BMD-20 RL	(USSR)	
	140 mm BM-14-16 RL	(USSR)	1300
	122 mm BM-21 RL	(USSR)	
	Frog-5 SSM	(USSR)	9
	37 mm/57 mm/85 mm/ 100 mm AA	(USSR)	5000
Anti-tank	82 mm RCL	(USSR)	
	57 mm to 100 mm	(USSR)	1500
Mortars	81 mm/120 mm/160 mm	(USSR)	9000
Infantry	USSR in origin, some minor North Korean modifications		

KOREA, REPUBLIC

Strength: 520 000
Reserves, 1 000 000
Military service: 2½ years
Background: The South Korean Army exists to maintain the frontier with North Korea and to resist invasion. Although the army has not carried out any major operations since 1953 there are continual incursions and frontier alarms. Two divisions were sent to Viet-Nam, at the request of the USA, and this war gave some active service experience to the troops who were rotated through the divisions. In addition to safeguarding the country the army also plays an important educational role through conscription and has made a large contribution to the increasing importance of South Korea.

Structure: The major part of the army is deployed along the frontier, which is divided into an East and a West zone, the latter having the greater concentration of troops since it shields the capital. The remainder of the country is made up of four district commands. The Army is organised along American lines and follows the US system of command and training. The overall structure is of three armies, both the First and Third being on the frontier and the Second looking after the remainder of the country and the training organisations. Training is largely centralised for the conscripts while regular officers are trained at an academy that closely copies West Point. The Homeland Reserve Forces are village guards, intended to combat guerrilla infiltration. In all, the South Korean Army is a large and capable army well able to defend the country. Its ability to launch a sustained offensive is more doubtful.

 1 mechanised division
17 infantry divisions
 2 independent armoured brigades
 5 special forces brigades
 2 AA brigades
 7 independent tank battalions
30 artillery battalions
 1 SSM brigade
 2 SAM brigades

Women's unit of the Republic of Korea Army. (MARS)

KOREA, REPUBLIC

Equipment: The Army was built up with American equipment, but a good deal is now made in South Korea. Nevertheless the basis remains US, and it is ageing steadily.

AFVs	Tanks	M47/48 medium	(USA)	800
		M60	(USA)	60
APCs		M113	(USA)	500
		FIAT 6614	(Italy)	20
SP guns		203 mm M110	(USA)	16
		175 mm M107	(USA)	12
		155 mm M109	(USA)	76
Artillery		203 mm M115	(USA)	⎫
		155 mm M114/59	(USA)	⎬ 2000
		105 mm M101	(USA)	⎭
		Honest John SSM	(USA)	
		40 mm AA	(USA/Sweden)	40
		Hawk SAM	(USA)	80
		Nike Hercules SAM	(USA)	14
Anti-tank		90 mm M36	(USA)	100
		76 mm M18	(USA)	80
		106 mm M40A1 RCL	(USA)	
		57 mm/75 mm RCL	(USA)	
		TOW ATGW	(USA)	
Mortars		81 mm/107 mm	(USA)	5300
Infantry		Entirely US in origin		

KUWAIT

Strength: 8500
Para-military forces 2000
Military service: 18 months
Background: The Kuwaiti army is not strong enough to be able to do more than provide minimal defence for the frontiers and to delay any aggressor who chose to invade. It has no real external role in the Gulf area other than providing a secure base for friendly countries to use should this ever be necessary. The army is organised on British lines, but the training is a mixture of several different nationalities. Recruitment for the regular cadre is difficult and conscription is not popular.
Structure: The small army is largely concentrated towards the frontier with Iraq. The units are very similar in size and make-up to their British counterparts.
1 armoured brigade
2 infantry brigades

KUWAIT

Equipment: There is no arms industry and all weapons and equipment are imported. Money is lavishly provided and though the army is light in artillery, it has adequate armoured vehicles and spares.

AFVs Tanks	Chieftain	(UK)	160
	Vickers	(UK)	70
	Centurion	(UK)	50
Armoured cars	Saladin	(UK)	100
cars	Ferret	(UK)	20
APC	Saracen	(UK)	130
SP guns	155 mm AMX	(France)	20
Anti-tank	SS11 ATGW	(France)	
	HOT ATGW	(France)	
	TOW ATGW	(USA)	
	Vigilant ATGW	(UK)	
Infantry	Largely French and Belgian in origin		

LAOS

Strength: 45 000 (estimated)

Military service: Conscription for an unknown period of time

Background: The People's Liberation Army of Laos (PLAL) is largely an unknown quantity in the West. It is thought to consist of about 100 infantry battalions with some supporting arms and services. The country is probably divided into military regions, perhaps five, and the troops are spread among them. The main role appears to be that of internal security and it is likely that training is indifferent and capabilities low.

Equipment: There is, or was, plenty of US equipment in Laotian hands and now there should be a mixture of French, Soviet and Chinese as well. Quantities are not known nor is there any indication of serviceability.

AFVs Tanks	M24	(USA)
	PT-76 light	(USSR)
APCs	M113	(USA)
	BTR-40	(USSR)
Artillery	75 mm M116 pack howitzers	(USA)
	105 mm & 155 mm howitzers	(USA & USSR)
Mortars	Various calibres	

LEBANON

Strength: 8000 (estimated)
Para-military forces, 5000 (Internal Security Police)
Military service: Conscription
Background: It is extremely difficult to produce a coherent picture of the present position of the army in Lebanon. The effects of the civil war are still very strong and Syria exercises almost as much weight in the internal affairs of the country as does the official government. There is much talk of expanding the army to a strength of at least 15 000, and if this came about it would relieve Syria of providing a peacekeeping army on the northern borders of Israel, but the cost is so great that it seems highly unlikely that it will ever happen. The conflict between Christian and Moslem largely nullifies the offensive capability of the army and it is little more effective than an armed gendarmerie.

Structure
2 armoured battalions
6 infantry battalions
2 artillery battalions
Equipment: There is no arms industry and all equipment is imported. The general position is that the army has a mixture of European and American weapons and vehicles and there are promises of more American items, though they come slowly.

AFVs Armoured cars	Saladin	(UK)
APCs	M113	(USA)
	Saracen	(UK)
Artillery	122 mm guns	(USSR)
	155 mm guns	(USA)
Anti-tank	MILAN ATGW	(France)

LIBERIA

Strength: 5200
Para-military forces, 7000-10 000
Military service: Voluntary
Background: Liberia sees an external threat to her independence from Guinea and one role of the army is undoubtedly to counter this, but the main task is to pacify the country and maintain the government of the day. Training is not good and the Militia is particularly low in competence.
Structure: The quoted number of units seems oddly at variance with the total strength and most of the units must be quite small.
5 infantry battalions
1 Presidential Guard battalion
1 engineer battalion
1 artillery battalion
1 service battalion
1 reconnaissance company

Equipment: There is no arms industry and all equipment is imported. Most is old and the state of maintenance is unknown.

AFVs Scout cars	M3A1	(USA)	12
Artillery	105 mm M2 howitzer	(USA)	
	75 mm M116 pack	(USA)	
Anti-tank	106 mm RCL	(USA)	
Mortars	81 mm M2	(USA)	
Infantry	Largely elderly US equipment		

LIBYA

Strength: 35 000
No apparent formed reserves or para-military forces
Military service: 18 months conscription
Background: Although the Libyan constitution declares that the army is maintained to safeguard the state, under Colonel Gaddafi it has become 'The arsenal of Islam' and the stated aim of the military forces is to defeat Israel. The wealth derived from oil allows the country to have armed forces far in excess of its needs and to indulge in minor adventures across its frontiers. So far these have been unsuccessful and costly.
Structure: The general organisation of the army used to be on British lines and this may have survived, but the training they receive is a mixture from Soviet, Cuban and French missions. The preponderance of armour to artillery is interesting.

1 armoured brigade
2 mechanised brigades
1 National Guard brigade
1 special forces brigade
2 AA battalions
2 artillery battalions

Equipment: Libya imports from different sources according to how her political credit stands at any one time. As a result the army must be a nightmare to supply and service.

AFVs Tanks	T-54/55/62	(USSR)	2000
Armoured cars	Saladin	(UK)	⎫ 100
	Panhard AML	(France)	⎭
	Cascavel EE-9	(Brazil)	200
	Ferret	(UK)	140
	Shorland	(UK)	
APCs	BTR-40/50/60	(USSR)	400
	BMP	(USSR)	200
	OT-64	(Czechoslovakia)	140
	Saracen	(UK)	70
	M113	(USA)	100
SP guns	155 mm M109	(USA)	40
Artillery	155 mm M114	(USA)	
	130 mm M46	(USSR)	80
	105 mm M101	(USA)	75
	Scud-B SSM	(USSR)	25
	Scaleboard SS-12 SSM	(USSR)	24
	23 mm ZSU-23-4 AA	(USSR)	
	57 mm AA	(USSR)	
	SA-7 SAM	(USSR)	
Anti-tank	106 mm M40A1 RCL	(USA)	
	Vigilant ATGW	(UK)	
Infantry	Mixture of Belgian, British, Italian and Soviet equipment		

LUXEMBOURG

Strength: 660
Reserves, 430 gendarmerie
Background: A founder member of NATO, Luxembourg maintains one infantry battalion by voluntary service and assigns it permanently to the ACE Mobile Force. It is a lightly-armed but well-trained element of the Force and is up to strength. There is a move to raise and equip another battalion. Despite the heavy industrial base in the country there is no arms industry and all equipment is imported and is of NATO patterns.

MADAGASCAR

Strength: 9500
Military service: 18 months
Background: Since independence the island of Madagascar has gone through several changes of government, all accompanied by more or less internal fighting. The army really exists to maintain internal security and the government of the day. It is therefore more of an armed gendarmerie and since there is virtually no external threat to the coastline there is no need for more than light arms and equipment. The state of training of the units is probably questionable, but it is apparently adequate for the tasks in hand. A more important objective for the armed forces is the general education of the population.

Structure
2 infantry regiments (nominally of 3 infantry battalions each)
1 engineer regiment
1 signals regiment
1 service battalion
Equipment: Practically all equipment is French, but there are some American vehicles.

AFVs	Armoured cars	M8	(USA)
	Scout cars	Ferret	(UK)
	APCs	M3A1 Half-track	(USA)

MALAWI

Strength: 5000
Military service: Voluntary
Background: Malawi was originally Nyasaland and the army is formed from the previous Nyasaland battalions of the King's African Rifles. The British traditions and training methods have survived and the main role of the army is to police the frontier.
Structure
3 infantry battalions (1, 2 & 3 The Malawi Rifles)
1 support battalion
Equipment: Practically all equipment is British and apart from the usual infantry weapons there are nine Ferret scout cars.

MALAYSIA

Strength: 52 000
Reserves, approximately 20 000
Military service: Voluntary
Background: The role of the army is to safeguard the country against attack and to maintain internal communications so that the government can effectively govern. Since the withdrawal of the British in the Far East there has been an increasing number of communist guerrilla attacks on Malaysia and other countries and as a result the army has been largely employed in border security. There is no question of the Malaysian Army being used for external operations and it is not equipped for such. The standard of training is good and largely based on British lines.

Structure: For some time the army has been organised on a two-divisional basis, but there has been talk of forming a third division.

2 divisional HQ
9 brigade HQ
29 infantry battalions
3 reconnaissance battalions
3 artillery battalions
2 AA batteries
1 special service unit
5 engineer battalions
4 signals regiments
Support and administrative units

Equipment: When Malaysia came into being in 1963 the forces were entirely equipped with British weapons. Since then there has been some diversion of source and in the field of infantry equipment there is quite a variety. There is no indigenous arms industry.

AFVs

Reconnaissance vehicles	Panhard AML	(France)	140
	Ferret	(UK)	60
	V-150 Commando	(USA)	200
Artillery	105 mm Model 56 pack	(Italy)	80
	40 mm LAA	(Sweden)	
Anti-tank	120 mm Wombat RCL	(UK)	
Mortars	81 mm L16A1	(UK)	
Infantry	A mixture of Belgian, British, German, Italian and US weapons		

MALI

Strength: 4000
Para-military forces, 5500
Military service: Voluntary
Background: On first gaining independence from France Mali decided to steer clear of French influence and soon drifted into the Soviet orbit. Much of the army training and equipment dates from this period. In more recent years a change of government has brought the French back more into favour but the army is still poorly trained and equipped. Border clashes with Upper Volta and other neighbours have not shown the troops in a good light, though some civic projects have gone well. The conscription time may be spent on civil projects instead of military service.
Structure: The highest operational formation is likely to be the battalion. The parachute company is almost certainly not trained nor capable of being flown by the air force.
5 infantry battalions
1 tank company
1 parachute company
1 artillery battalion
1 engineer company

Equipment: Most of the equipment is elderly and probably in a poor state of repair. There is no money to buy more and no country apart from the USSR willing to provide it free.

AFVs Tanks		T-34	(USSR)	24
		Type 62 light	(PRC)	6
Armoured cars		BRDM-2	(USSR)	20
APCs		BTR-40/152	(USSR)	10
Artillery		100 mm M1955	(USSR)	
		85 mm D-44	(USSR)	
		23 mm/37 mm/57 mm LAA	(USSR)	
Mortars		81/120 mm	(USSR)	

MALTA

Strength: 1000
Military service: Voluntary
Background: The Maltese Army has no really viable role beyond that of internal security and aid to the civil power. The state of training and equipment is not clear.
Structure
1 infantry battalion
1 engineer battalion

MAURITANIA

Strength: 9000
Reserves, 6000
Military service: Voluntary
Background: After a long period of comparative peace the Mauritanian Army became involved in a guerrilla war with the Polisario. The advantage lay with the guerrillas, and the Mauritanians lost prestige and spirit. They are now recovering, but the strength of the army has had to be cut because of budget restrictions. The general shape and training of the army is French and most of the equipment is similarly French.
Structure
30 motorised infantry companies (approximately)
  1 parachute-commando company (no capability to parachute)
  3 reconnaissance squadrons
  1 artillery battery
Equipment
AFVs

Armoured cars	EBR-75	(France)	} 15
	AML-90	(France)	
No artillery			
Mortars	81 & 120 mm	(France)	

MEXICO

Strength: 80 000
Reserves, 250 000 partly-trained conscripts
Military service: Voluntary
Background: The Mexican Army is in many ways quite unlike other South American armies. It is theoretically conscript but in fact is manned by regulars and the militia absorbs the conscript element. The main role is to maintain internal peace, especially at election times when feelings run high. There is almost no threat to the frontiers and no call for expansion. As a result the army is scarcely able to mount any form of modern operation.
Structure: Most of the regular army consists of battalion sized units stationed in the larger cities. Operationally the largest formation is the brigade, of which there are three.
 1 mechanised brigade group (Presidential Guard)
 2 infantry brigade groups
 1 parachute brigade
Independent units stationed in cities:
 23 independent cavalry regiments
 64 independent infantry battalions
   Artillery, engineer and support units

Equipment: There is a small arms industry in Mexico which manufactures for its own forces, but does not export. The great majority of the weapons are old, though serviceable.

AFVs Tanks	M3/5 Stuart	(USA)
	M4 Sherman	(USA)
Armoured cars	M3A1	(USA)
	M8	(USA)
APCs	HWK 11	(West Germany)
	M3 half-track	(USA)
SP guns	105 mm M8	(USA)
	75 mm M7	(USA)
Artillery	105 mm M101	(USA)
	75 mm M116 pack	(USA)
Infantry	Mixture of Mexican design and manufacture and US imports	

West German HWK 11 APCs awaiting shipment to Mexico in 1964. (C. Foss)

MONGOLIA

Strength: 27 000
Para-military forces, approximately 18 000 frontier guards
Military service: Two years
Background: Mongolia is a buffer state between the USSR and China and its huge size and small population make it quite impossible for it to defend itself. The army is largely a national symbol, urged on it by the Soviets who supply all the equipment and the training.
Structure: The locations of the army are quite unknown, but are probably along the frontiers where they act as a sort of border guard.
2 infantry divisions (roughly-brigade strength)
1 construction brigade (usually employed on civil projects)

Equipment

AFVs	Tanks	T-34	(USSR)	30
		T-54/55	(USSR)	100
APCs		BTR-60/152	(USSR)	80
Artillery		152 mm D-1	(USSR)	
		130 mm M46	(USSR)	
		100 mm M1944/55	(USSR)	
		76 mm M1942	(USSR)	
		37 mm and 57 mm LAA	(USSR)	
Anti-tank		57 mm M-43	(USSR)	
		Snapper ATGW	(USSR)	
Infantry		Entirely Soviet in origin		

The Mongolian Army uses these BTR-60P APCs. All equipment is supplied by the Soviet Union. (C. Foss)

MOROCCO

Strength: 80 000
Military service: Voluntary
Background: The principal roles of the army are internal security and the resistance of external aggression. It has been concentrating on the latter in recent years with the threat from the Polisario guerrillas and Moroccan troops have been sent to assist Mauritania in its struggle. In addition there are Moroccan troops in Zaïre and units have served with some of the UN peacekeeping forces. The standard of training is relatively good, though hampered by the different types of equipment, however the policy is to keep to the simpler weapons and tactics. This approach seems to have worked well so far.

Structure: There is an ever-present danger of political coups so the army is kept fragmented and spread out. As a result it is difficult to produce a coherent pattern of deployment within the country. The Royal Guard is kept separate from the main army. It would appear from the actions against the Polisario that the operational staff do not commit larger forces than battalions at one time.

1 light security brigade
1 parachute brigade (virtually no capability for dropping)
5 armoured battalions
9 motorised infantry battalions
18 infantry battalions
2 Royal Guard battalions
7 camel battalions
2 desert cavalry battalions
7 artillery groups (size varies)
2 engineer battalions

Morocco uses a large number of French supplied VAB 6 × 6 APCs.

MOROCCO

Equipment: There is no arms industry and since the policy for equipment has changed over the years the supply and maintenance of this mixture must be difficult. The French equipment was inherited originally, the American came next under a military aid programme, and the Soviet was last of all. Spares must be scarce for some items.

AFVs	Tanks	M48	(USA)	100
		T-54	(USSR)	40
		AMX-13	(France)	80
Armoured cars		EBR-75	(France)	36
		AML-90	(France)	
		M8	(USA)	50
APCs		VAB	(France)	
		M3 half-track	(USA)	40
		OT-64	(Czechoslovakia)	60
		UR-416	(West Germany)	30
		M113	(USA)	110
SP guns		155 mm M109	(USA)	36
		105 mm AMX	(France)	20

Artillery	152 mm M1937	(USSR)
	105 mm M101	(USA)
	85 mm D-44	(USSR)
	76 mm M1942	(USSR)
	75 mm M116 pack	(USA)
	57 mm AA	(USSR)
	40 mm LAA	(Sweden)
	23 mm ZSU-23-4 LAA	(USSR)
	Chaparral SAM	(USA)
	Crotale SAM	(France)
Anti-tank	TOW ATGW	(USA)
	Dragon ATGW	(USA)
Infantry	Mixture of French, Italian and some Soviet weapons. The French predominate in all categories	

MOZAMBIQUE

Strength: up to 20 000
Military service: Two years
Background: The FRELIMO government of Mozambique seems intent on setting up a Marxist state and information on the armed forces is hard to come by. However, it is thought that there has been a large build-up in numbers and equipment in the past two years and that Cuban, Soviet and East German advisers are active in the country.
Structure: The best information is that there are four 'divisions' in the army, but of what strength and make-up is not known. It is certain that they must be small divisions and are probably not more than brigades.

Equipment: Although infantry weapons and small arms appear to be a fair mixture of nationalities the heavier items are almost without exception of Soviet origin. There have been shipments into Maputo and Nacala recently. The following list is not necessarily based on actual sightings.

AFVs Tanks	T-34/54/55	(USSR)	200+
	PT-76 light	(USSR)	some
Armoured cars	BRDM	(USSR)	
APCs	BTR-40/50	(USSR)	
Artillery	152 mm D-1	(USSR)	
	122 mm M1938	(USSR)	
	100 mm M1955	(USSR)	
	85 mm D-44	(USSR)	
	76 mm M1942	(USSR)	
Anti-tank	107 mm B-11 RCL	(USSR)	
	Sagger ATGW	(USSR)	

NEPAL

Strength: 20 000
Military service: Voluntary
Background: The Nepalese army is a separate force from those ghurkas who emigrate and serve in either the British or Indian armies. The national army stays within its frontiers and acts as a combined police and border guard. It is extremely well-trained and disciplined and it plays no part in national politics. Essentially it is a collection of units and a soldier joins a battalion in which he stays for his military life. Although too small to do much more than slow down an aggressor, the army would be able to prevent an overnight invasion and hold on until international opinion was mobilised.

Structure
5 infantry brigades (one is a palace guard)
1 parachute battalion
1 artillery regiment
1 engineer regiment
1 signals regiment

Equipment: All equipment has to be imported through India and most is bought there. However, the majority of equipment is light and portable enough for mountain warfare.

AFVs Tanks	AMX-13 light	(France)	
Artillery	3.7 in pack	(UK)	4
	40 mm LAA	(UK/Sweden)	2
Mortars	120 mm	(France)	
	4.2 in	(UK)	

Nepal is one of the last users of the British 3.7-in mountain howitzer.

NETHERLANDS

Strength: 75 000 (43 000 conscripts)
Reserves, 140 000+
Military service: 14 months
Background: The Royal Netherlands Army has a long history and a reputation for determined fighting in defence of its country. The role of the modern army is to provide a corps of three divisions to NATO, to defend the nation and to provide the logistical support for both activities. Since about two-thirds of the army is composed of conscripts their training is an additional and constant burden. There has been much debate about the attitude of the Dutch conscripts, many of whom have shown a marked anti-military tendency, but this has been muted in the last year or two. The difficulties with the army probably spring from the fact that with the exception of an armoured brigade and some other units in West Germany, all troops spend their time in barracks in the Netherlands.

Structure
2 armoured brigades
4 mechanised infantry brigades
1 SSM brigade (Lance)

Gepard self-propelled anti-aircraft gun of the Royal Netherlands Army.

Equipment: Despite a flourishing motor and electronics industry the Netherlands does not manufacture much in the way of weapons and most is imported from other NATO countries. Maintenance standards are excellent.

AFVs	Tanks	Leopard 1	(West Germany)	400
		Centurion	(UK)	330
		AMX-13 light	(France)	120
	APCs	AMX-VC1	(France)	1300
		M113	(USA)	
		YP-408	(Netherlands)	750
		YP-765	(Netherlands)	860
SP guns		203 mm M110	(USA)	
		175 mm M107	(USA)	24
		155 mm M109	(USA)	80
		105 mm AMX	(France)	48
Artillery		203 mm M115	(USA)	
		155 mm M114	(USA)	
		105 mm M101	(USA)	
		Lance SSM	(USA)	6
		Gepard SP AA	(West Germany)	45
Anti-tank		106 mm M40A1 RCL	(USA)	
		TOW ATGW	(USA)	
Mortars		120 mm	(France)	
Infantry		UZI SMG	(Israel)	
		FAL rifle	(Belgium)	
		MAG MG	(Belgium)	

143

NEW ZEALAND

Strength: 5600
Reserves, 1500 regular, 6000 TA
Military service: Voluntary
Background: The New Zealand Army has an honourable place in Commonwealth history for its participation in the wars of this century. It is recruited by a unique method combining a small regular force with a part-time Territorial Army (TA) which undertakes unusually long training periods each year and which is always ready to turn out and supplement the regulars. The role of the army is to safeguard the state from external aggression, to safeguard the essential communications around New Zealand, to contribute in times of war to the collective defence of the areas vital to New Zealand and to contribute as appropriate towards UN forces. The method of carrying out this large task is to keep the majority of the army at home, but ready to move at short notice. The army is highly-trained and well motivated, it has had recent experience in Viet-Nam and in several civil projects in the Pacific area.

Structure: There are two commands, Home which provides the home support for the army in the country and the Field Force Command which is structured to provide a brigade sized formation for deployment in a crisis. This force would be made up from the TA though it has a regular cadre who keep it in being.
2 infantry battalions
1 artillery regiment
Equipment: There is a very small capability to manufacture small arms and ammunition, but all other items are imported—traditionally from UK but more recently from USA and Australia.

AFVs Tanks	M41 light	(USA)	5
Scout cars	Ferret	(UK)	9
APCs	M113	(USA)	66
Artillery	5.5 in medium gun	(UK)	17
	105 mm Model 56 pack	(Italy)	41
Anti-tank	106 mm M40A1 RCL	(USA)	23
Infantry	All weapons and equipment are very similar to those of the British Army		

M41A1 light tank of the Royal New Zealand Armoured Corps, soon to be replaced by Scorpions.
(New Zealand Army/MARS)

NICARAGUA

Strength: 8000
Reserves, approximately 4000
Military service: Voluntary
Background: The defence forces in Nicaragua are known as the National Guard and the army is one element in it. The declared main task of the army is the maintenance of internal security and all other responsibilities come after that. The many political disturbances in the country, including the recent revolution, have not increased the popularity of the army among the peasants, who have been often treated with great severity. The army could not mount a conventional military operation, but it could defend the frontiers for some time if the country was invaded. There is no capability to mount an aggressive attack.
Structure: The Presidential Guard and the artillery and mechanised unit are kept in the capital. The independent companies are quartered in the towns, where they act as an armed back-up to the police.

 1 battalion Presidential Guard
 1 infantry battalion
16 independent infantry companies
 1 engineer battalion
 1 artillery battery
 1 AA battery

Equipment: There is no arms industry and all equipment is imported, originally from the USA, but in recent years from Israel. There have been announcements that Taiwan will help with material assistance.

AFVs Tanks	M4 Sherman	(USA)	
Armoured cars	T17E1 Staghound	(USA)	60
	M3A1	(USA)	3
Artillery	105 mm M101	(USA)	4
	40 mm LAA	(USA/Sweden)	8
Infantry	Predominantly US, but some Swiss SG540 rifles have been bought		

NIGER

Strength: 2000
Probably no formed reserves
Military service: Two years selective conscription
Background: This very small former French colony is both poor and helpless. The tiny army is used mainly to safeguard internal security and relations with the neighbouring states are good. Training and equipment is predominantly French and the state of maintenance of both weapons and vehicles is questionable.
1 reconnaissance squadron
5 infantry companies
1 parachute (sic) company
1 engineer company
Equipment
AFVs

Armoured cars	M8	(USA)	} 10
	M20	(USA)	
Mortars	81 mm	(France)	

NIGERIA

Strength: 160 000
No formed reserves
Military service: Voluntary
Background: Nigeria has not found it easy to convert from colonial rule to independence and one difficulty has been inter-tribal jealousy and feuding. For many years after the Biafran War the army was far too large, the largest in Black Africa, but a firm policy of retrenchment has brought it down to 160 000 which is probably as low as it can go for the present. Training has suffered due to the huge expansion in the early 1970s and this will take some time to put right, meanwhile the main task of the army is to stabilise the internal affairs of the country and to maintain the peace.
Structure: The main structure is based on four infantry divisions on the British model. HQs of both divisions and brigades are in the main towns but there is no overt territorial attachment between the army and particular sections of the country.
4 infantry divisions
4 artillery brigades
4 engineer brigades
4 reconnaissance regiments

NIGERIA

Equipment: Traditionally Nigeria has imported its equipment from the UK but this has been modified and now there is a spread of nationalities among all natures of weapons and equipment which must make maintenance difficult.

AFVs

Armoured cars	Scorpion tracked reconnaissance	(UK)	50
	Saladin	(UK)	20
	AML-60/90	(France)	15
Scout cars	Ferret	(UK)	25
	Fox	(UK)	50
APCs	Saracen	(UK)	8
Artillery	130 mm M46	(USSR)	
	122 mm D-74	(USSR)	
	105 mm Model 56 pack	(UK)	
	76 mm M1942	(USSR)	
	40 mm LAA	(UK/Sweden)	
Infantry	Mixture of British, West German and Italian		

NORWAY

Strength: 20 000 (17 500 conscripts)
Reserves, 120 000
Military service: One year
Background: Norway is one of the European countries with a policy of a 'nation in arms' and the defence forces are closely integrated into national life. All able-bodied men are expected to turn out in time of war and defend the country and there is every indication that they would do so. The army is earmarked to NATO and trains frequently with NATO allies. The country has one of the two NATO borders with the USSR and there is an ever-present danger of invasion over it into Finnmark. The army is unlikely to mount operations outside its national boundaries, but it could offer a redoubtable defence if attacked. Norway makes considerable contributions to UN peacekeeping forces.

Structure: The country is divided into Northern and Southern Commands. The training centres and most of the population are in the south. There is a brigade stationed in the north and local defence forces and mobilisation centres are in the towns. The Home Guard is further broken down into local areas.

1 brigade group (Northern Norway)
Independent armoured squadrons, infantry battalions and artillery regiments
1 battalion group in Lebanon

Norwegian Home Guard on winter manoeuvres. (C. Foss)

NORWAY

Equipment: The Kongsberg and Raufoss factories manufacture light weapons and ammunition but the majority of heavier equipment is imported and conforms to NATO patterns.

AFVs	Tanks	Leopard I	(West Germany)	78
		M48 medium	(USA)	38
		NM-116	(USA/Norway)	70
APCs		M113	(USA)	
SP guns		155 mm M109	(USA)	130
Artillery		155 mm M114	(USA)	250
		105 mm M101	(USA)	
		20 mm Rh 202 LAA	(West Germany)	
Anti-tank		106 mm M40A1 RCL	(USA)	
		ENTAC ATGW	(France)	
		TOW ATGW	(USA)	
Mortars		107 mm M30/M30F1	(USA/Norway)	
		81 mm NM95	(UK/Norway)	
Infantry		Mainly licence-built designs from other NATO countries		

OMAN

Strength: 16,200
Military service: Voluntary
Background: Oman's army has passed through a four-fold expansion since 1970 and there is still a need for time to settle and assimilate the changes. Although still largely led by British and Pakistani officers and senior NCOs the time is not far distant when the majority of officers will be Omanis. Training is good and the long war with the Dhofar guerrillas has given all plenty of operational experience. Battalions are still rotated through Dhofar and the danger is still present. The army is not capable of launching any major offensives, but it can defend the frontiers against guerrilla infiltration and maintain internal stability in the country itself.

Rapier anti-aircraft unit of the Omani Army.
(British Aerospace)

OMAN

Structure: The infantry battalions are rotated between the northern command and the Dhofar Brigade. The highest operational formation is the brigade, which does operate as such.
2 brigade HQ
8 infantry battalions
1 Royal Guard battalion
1 artillery regiment
1 signals regiment
1 armoured car squadron
1 parachute squadron
1 engineer squadron
Equipment: Most of the equipment is British and all is imported.

AFVs

Armoured cars	Saladin	(UK)	36
	AT-105	(Ireland)	
Scout cars	Ferret	(UK)	
APCs	V-150 Commando	(USA)	
Artillery	105 mm Model 56 pack	(UK/Italy)	36
Anti-tank	TOW ATGW	(USA)	
Mortars	81 mm L16A1	(UK)	
	107 mm M30	(USA)	
Infantry	Very similar to that of UK		

PAKISTAN

Strength: 400 000
Reserves, approximately 500 000
Military service: Voluntary
Background: The main role of the army is the defence of the country against India. There is also the possible threat of incursion from Afghanistan, made the more likely since the Soviet invasion of that country. The army has also been used for several internal security operations, some quite large. It has fought three wars since 1948 and much active service has been passed in internal fighting. The army has retained much of the British regimental system and recruits will usually stay in their regiment for their entire service life. There is a large regular reserve and an ambitious scheme to provide a Home Guard for the entire country.

Structure: The structure of the army is inherited from the British and consists of divisions and brigades. For operations more than one division will be grouped into a corps and the staff to man these HQ exist and are trained. There seems to be no fixed distribution of units around the country in peacetime, but it is understood that there is a majority of troops in Punjaub and Scind where there has been some civil disturbance.

2 armoured divisions
16 infantry divisions
3 independent armoured brigades
3 independent infantry brigades
6 artillery brigades
2 AA brigades
5 army aviation squadrons

Equipment: The arms industry is state-run and is capable of repair, maintenance and the manufacture of ammunition and spare parts. However, there is steady expansion and in time Pakistan will be able to make most of her needs herself. Meanwhile she suffers from a mixture of equipment of all ages.

AFVs	Tanks			
		M4 Sherman	(USA)	
		M24 Chaffee	(USA)	50
		M47/48	(USA)	250
		T-54/55	(USSR)	50
		Type 59	(PRC)	700
		Type 63 light	(PRC)	
		PT-76 light	(USSR)	
APCs		M113	(USA)	550
SP guns		155 mm M109	(USA)	
		105 mm M7	(USA)	12
		90 mm M36 ATk	(USA)	8

PAKISTAN

Artillery	155 mm M59/114	(USA)	
	5.5 in medium gun	(UK)	
	130 mm Type 59	(PRC)	
	105 mm M101	(USA)	
	105 mm Model 56 pack	(UK/Italy)	1000
	100 mm Type 59	(PRC)	
	25 pdr	(UK)	
	75 mm M116 pack	(USA)	
	90 mm M117 AA	(USA)	15
	3.7 in AA	(UK)	
	40 mm LAA	(UK/Sweden)	
	30 mm/37 mm/ 57 mm LAA	(USSR)	
	Crotale SAM	(France)	9
Anti-tank	17 pdr gun	(UK)	
	106 mm M40A1 RCL	(USA)	
	Cobra ATGW	(West Germany)	
Mortars	120 mm	(USSR)	
	81 mm M29	(USA)	
Infantry	Mixture of British, Chinese, West German and US weapons		

PANAMA

Strength: 11 000 (about 5000 predominantly army)
Military service: Voluntary
Background: The National Guard is a combination of police and military forces and it probably comes nearer to a gendarmerie than any other South American army. Its sole function is the maintenance of law and order in the country and all external defence is left to the USA. The force is distributed throughout the country, but more than half is in Panama City and the purely military elements are rarely brought together into one body. The equipment is almost entirely American and consists of light weapons and some armoured cars.

PAPUA–NEW GUINEA

Strength: 3500
Military service: Voluntary
Background: The functions of the small defence force of Papua-New Guinea are firstly to defend the country and secondly to give all aid to the civil power in the event of a disaster or a breakdown of public order. In fact their main role would be to act as a guarantee of national unity in a country in which there are many tribal differences. External defence is more or less assured by Australia and apart from guerrilla activity along the frontier with West Irian there is no overt threat to the country at all. The small army is organised along British lines and is equipped with light arms made in, or purchased by, Australia.

Structure
2 infantry battalions
1 engineer battalion
1 signals battalion
 small logistic units

PARAGUAY

Strength: 12 500
Reserves, approximately 400 000, though not organised as such
Military service: 1½ years
Background: The country is a stable military dictatorship and much of the effort of the army is directed to maintaining the government in power. It also takes part in civil developments and engineering projects. Through conscription it makes a useful contribution to the education of the peasants and generally assists the police in upholding internal law and order. By and large training is elementary and never above unit level and the military capability of the army is very limited.

PARAGUAY

Structure: The country is divided into six divisional areas with a battalion in each. The additional troops are in and around the capital though the engineers are sent to wherever they are needed for particular projects.

1 cavalry "division" (not above brigade strength)
6 infantry "divisions" (each about a battalion strong)
2 independent horsed cavalry regiments (may be in the cavalry division)
2 independent infantry battalions
1 Presidential Guard (battalion)
1 artillery regiment
5 engineer regiments
1 signals battalion

Equipment: There is no attempt to manufacture any arms in Paraguay and everything is imported. The state of readiness of any of the vehicles is questionable.

AFVs Tanks	M4 Sherman	(USA)	9
	M3A1 light	(USA)	12
APCs	M113	(USA)	some
Artillery	105 mm M101	(USA)	48
	75 mm M116 pack	(USA)	
	40 mm LAA	(USA/Sweden)	
Infantry	Mixture of Belgian, Danish, Swiss and US weapons		

PERU

Strength: 70 000 (49 000 conscripts)
Para-military forces, 25 000 Civil Guards
Military service: Two years selective conscription
Background: Peru is another South American dictatorship and the army is deeply and closely involved in the government of the country. Whether this is a good or a bad thing is hard to say. Officers are actually integrated into the government and it is not easy at times to separate the two functions. However, the army does maintain some distinct military tasks. One is the maintenance of internal security and another the security of the frontiers. The engineers, as so often in South America, are involved in civil projects but the military does not see itself as an educational force in the nation. This may be because the conscription is selective by ballot and does not affect all men. Although there is a reserve obligation for all conscripts it does not seem to be enforced or organised. The capability of the army is limited to minor actions, largely defensive in character.

Structure: The dispositions of the army are not easy to discover. There has been some increase in the strength in recent years, but the practice of describing as 'divisions' formations which are no more than battalions leads to confusion.

2 armoured divisions (brigade strength)
1 cavalry division (2 armoured regiments and 2 horsed regiments)
8 infantry and mechanised divisions (brigades)
1 'para-commando' division (brigade)
1 jungle division (brigade)
3 armoured reconnaissance squadrons
  Artillery batteries
  Engineer companies

Equipment: Peru has been able to buy her equipment using her indigenous raw materials as exchange and her traditional supplier has been the USA. But in the 1970s a move away from America led to purchases from the USSR with the result that the army now has a mixture of equipment with the consequent maintenance and spares troubles that this brings.

AFVs Tanks		T-54/55	(USSR)	250
		M4 Sherman	(USA)	60
		AMX-13 light	(France)	110
Armoured cars		M8	(USA)	
Scout cars		M3A1	(USA)	50
APCs		M113	(USA)	
		V-200 Chaimite	(Portugal)	
		UR-416	(West Germany)	200
		MOWAG Roland	(Switzerland)	
Artillery		155 mm M114	(USA)	
		130 mm M46	(USSR)	
		122 mm D-74	(USSR)	
		105 mm M101	(USA)	
		40 mm LAA	(USA/Sweden)	
		23 mm ZSU-23-4 LAA	(USSR)	80
		SA-7 SAM	(USSR)	
Anti-tank		Cobra ATGW	(West Germany)	
Mortars		120 mm		
Infantry		Mixture of Belgian, West German and some Soviet weapons		

PHILIPPINES

Strength: 65 000
Reserves, 12 000
Military service: Voluntary, aided by selective conscription
Background: The role of the army is to preserve the territorial integrity of the 7000 islands which make up the Republic. The USA is committed to the defence of the Philippines against external aggression (in return for the use of bases) and thus the army can concentrate on maintaining internal security and in controlling the several dissident groups who are at odds with the central government. The southern islands are particularly turbulent. Training is probably sketchy since it is largely carried out in the recruit's unit, but there is a military academy for officers. The engineer units are used to improve the civil amenities in the interior and for all arms the highest operational formation would appear to be the individual unit.

Structure: Although there are divisions and brigades it is thought that these are more logistical than operational groupings.
4 light infantry divisions
1 independent infantry brigade (awaiting mechanisation)
Equipment: A small industrial base is capable of manufacturing light weapons and ammunition, but all other equipment has to be imported, almost all from the USA.

AFVs Tanks	M41 light	(USA)	7
Reconnaissance vehicles	Scorpion	(UK)	28
APCs	M113	(USA)	60
	V-150 Commando	(USA)	20
Artillery	155 mm M114	(USA)	6
	105 mm M101	(USA)	120
	Hawk SAM	(USA)	
Anti-tank	106 mm M40A1 RCL	(USA)	
Mortars	107 mm (4.2 in) M2A1	(USA)	
	81 mm M1	(USA)	
Infantry	Some West German rifles, but otherwise all US in origin		

POLAND

Strength: 210 000 (150 000 conscripts)
Reserves, 500 000
Military service: Two years
Background: The army has the twin responsibilities of the defence of the country and the maintenance of internal security. The latter is obviously the more important since the country is surrounded by fellow members of the Warsaw Pact. The army is entirely based and trained on Soviet lines.
Structure: The structure of the army is so close to the Soviet model that it is not worthwhile to repeat it in detail. Polish troops do not serve outside the country, though a few took part in the invasion of Czechoslovakia in 1968.
5 tank divisions
8 motor rifle divisions
1 airborne division
1 amphibious assault division
4 SSM brigades (Scud)
3 artillery brigades
1 independent artillery regiment
5 independent AA regiments
3 anti-tank regiments

Polish troops loading Snapper ATGW. (I. V. Hogg)

Equipment: Poland manufactures light weapons and ammunition and some use is made of Czechoslovak-made equipment. Otherwise all items are imported from the USSR.

AFVs

Tanks	T-54/55 medium	(USSR)	3400
	PT-76 light	(USSR)	300
Scout cars	OT-65	(Czechoslovakia)	
	BRDM-1/2	(USSR)	} 2000
APCs	BMP	(USSR)	5500
	OT-62/64	(Czechoslovakia)	
SP guns	122 mm M-1974	(USSR)	
	85 mm ASU-85	(USSR)	

Artillery	152 mm D-1/M1937	(USSR)	250
	130 mm M46	(USSR)	
	122 mm D-30/D-74/ M1931/M1938	(USSR)	} 400
	100 mm M1944/55	(USSR)	
	76 mm M1942	(USSR)	
	140 mm BM-14-16/ 17 RL	(USSR)	} 250
	122 mm BM-21 RL	(USSR)	
	Frog SSM	(USSR)	52
	Scud SSM	(USSR)	36
	23 mm, 57 mm, 85 mm, 100 mm AA	(USSR)	400
	ZSU-23-4 LAA	(USSR)	100
	ZSU-57-2 LAA	(USSR)	24
	SA-6/9 SAM	(USSR)	
Anti-tank	82 mm, 107 mm RCL	(USSR)	
	Snapper, Sagger ATGW	(USSR)	
Mortars	120 mm M1943	(USSR)	

Polish rocket troops loading BM21 launcher. (I. V. Hogg)

PORTUGAL

Strength: 37 000
Para-military forces, 31 500 National Guard and Police
Military service: 16 months
Background: The army is still not completely recovered from the unsettling loss of the colonial war in Africa and the political upheavals which followed. Portugal is an enthusiastic member of NATO and is forming a special brigade to be assigned to it. Recruit training is good and is started centrally in a Recruit School and completed in the man's unit. Although there is a residual commitment to reserve service, this has so far never been implemented and is a paper exercise.
Structure: The country is divided into regional commands with formations in each and there is a move to integrate formations and units with their local areas.

1 infantry brigade (NATO)
1 tank regiment
2 cavalry regiments
16 infantry regiments
1 commando regiment
4 independent infantry battalions
3 artillery regiments
1 coast artillery regiment
1 AA regiment
2 engineer regiments
1 signals regiment

Portugese artillerymen with M101 105 mm howitzer. (I. V. Hogg)

Equipment: There is an arms industry which produces light arms and ammunition and exports a good proportion. Heavier equipment is either British or US.

AFVs	Tanks	M47 medium	(USA)	34
		M48 medium	(USA)	30
		M24 light	(USA)	
	Armoured cars	Saladin	(UK)	
		AML	(France)	
	APCs	M113	(USA)	86
		Chaimite	(Portugal)	79
		EBR-ETT	(France)	36
		M3 Half-track	(USA)	
	SP guns	25 pdr Sexton	(UK)	
		105 mm M7	(USA)	
Artillery		155 mm M114	(USA)	
		5.5 in medium gun	(UK)	30
		105 mm M101	(USA)	130
		25 pdr	(UK)	
Anti-tank		106 mm M40A1 RCL	(USA)	
		TOW ATGW	(USA)	
Mortars		120 mm	(France)	
		81 mm/60 mm	(Portugal)	
Infantry		Almost all of Portuguese manufacture. Some Heckler & Koch designs made under licence		

QATAR

Strength: 4000
Military service: Voluntary
Background: The size of the country and the limited population make it impossible for the Qatar army to do more than deter any potential aggressor by the fact of its presence. However, it is supported by the remarkable oil income that flows into the government and is extremely well equipped and able to hire good training teams. The main role would seem to be that of internal security only.

Structure

2 armoured car regiments
1 guards infantry battalion
1 mobile regiment

Equipment: All equipment is imported, mostly from Europe and is well provided with spares and consumable items. The nature of the country has required a preponderance of vehicles and practically all troops are mechanised or motorised.

AFVs Tanks	AMX-30 medium	(France)	30
Armoured cars	Saladin	(UK)	30
	EE-9 Cascavel	(Brazil)	20
Scout cars	Ferret	(UK)	10
APCs	AMX-10P	(France)	12
	Saracen	(UK)	8
Artillery	25 pdr	(UK)	4
	105 mm light gun	(UK)	
Mortars	81 mm L16A1	(UK)	
Infantry	Variety of different nationalities, from both sides of the Iron Curtain		

ROMANIA

Strength: 140 000 (95 000 conscripts)
Reserves, 450 000
Military service: 16 months
Background: Romania is a member of the Warsaw Pact, but it has shown a degree of independence that is unusual among the Pact, and Romania has not always followed the Soviet lead in military matters. However, the army takes part in all WP exercises and would undoubtedly fall in with WP mobilisation and war plans. All troops are stationed within the national borders and they have not taken part in any operations since the end of the Second World War.

Structure: The divisions are grouped into three corps which coincide with a military district. There is probably no attempt to ensure any permanent link between the troops and the local population, but it is highly likely that recruit training takes place close to the recruit's home area.
2 tank divisions
8 motor rifle divisions
3 mountain brigades
1 airborne regiment
2 SSM brigades (Scud)
2 artillery brigade HQ
3 artillery regiments
2 AA regiments
2 anti-tank regiments

ROMANIA

Equipment: There is a small arms industry, but practically all weapons and equipment are imported and are from the USSR.

AFVs Tanks	T-34	(USSR)	200
	T-54/55	(USSR)	1300
Scout cars	BRDM	(USSR)	800
APCs	BTR-50/60	(USSR)	1500
	TAB-70/72	(USSR/Romania)	
SP guns	100 mm SU-100	(USSR)	130

Artillery	152 mm M1937/ M1938	(USSR)	150
	122 mm D-30/ D-74/M1931/ M1938	(USSR)	600
	100 mm M1944	(USSR)	
	85 mm D-44	(USSR)	50
	76 mm M1942	(USSR)	60
	130 mm M51 RL	(USSR)	150
	Frog SSM	(USSR)	30
	Scud SSM	(USSR)	20
	85 mm, 100 mm AA	(USSR)	250
	30 mm, 57 mm LAA	(USSR)	400
	SA-6/7 SAM	(USSR)	
Anti-tank	57 mm M1943	(USSR)	
	73 mm, 82 mm RCL	(USSR)	260
	Sagger, Snapper ATGW	(USSR)	120
Mortars	82 mm, 120 mm	(USSR)	1000
Infantry	Soviet in origin, sometimes with local variations		

RWANDA

Strength: 3600
Military service: Voluntary
Background: The tiny country of Rwanda is entirely land-locked, but is not so far threatened by its neighbours and the small army is only intended for internal security duties. There is a small Belgian training team and it is likely that the standard of military ability is low.
Structure
1 reconnaissance squadron
8 infantry companies
1 'commando' company
Equipment: All equipment is old, even by African standards and the state of readiness is uncertain.
AFVs

Armoured cars	AML-60/90	(France)	12
Anti-tank	6 pdr	(UK)	6
Mortars	81 mm	(France)	8
Infantry	French in origin		

SAUDI ARABIA

Strength: 35 000
Para-military forces, National Guard 25 000, Militia 15 000
Military service: Voluntary
Background: The role of the army is to maintain the integrity of the national frontiers and to protect the country from invasion. In times of internal strife the army would combine with the National Guard to maintain peace and this it did when dissidents took over the mosque in Mecca. The army is compact, well equipped and trained to a good professional standard by foreign teams, some of whom are very large. The question that must be answered in the next few years is the ability of the army to maintain its very complex technical equipment and to retain suitable motivation in the face of competition from a high standard of living and soaring wages in industry.
Structure: The army is entirely based in the country, mostly in a few large and expensive barrack complexes. Apart from small excursions against Israel in past years no units have been outside Arabia.
1 armoured brigade
4 infantry brigades
2 parachute battalions
1 Royal Guard battalion
3 artillery battalions
6 AA batteries
10 SAM batteries (Hawk)

SAUDI ARABIA

Equipment: There is a plant which manufactures small arms and ammunition under licence and it is planned to increase this capability in unison with the Arab Organisation for Industrialisation (AOI). Meanwhile equipment is imported and Saudi Arabia is so rich that she has two different nationalities of MBT. There are also other mixtures among the weaponry which must complicate supply and maintenance.

AFVs Tanks	AMX-30	(France)	250
	M60	(USA)	100
			(more on order)
Armoured cars	AML-60/90	(France)	⎫ 200
	Ferret	(UK)	⎭
	Fox	(UK)	50
APCs	AMX-10P	(France)	150
	M113	(USA)	200
	M3 Panhard	(France)	
SP guns	155 mm Mk F3	(France)	
	105 mm	(France)	
	40 mm M42 SPAA	(USA)	
	30 mm AMX-30 SPAA	(France)	

Artillery	105 mm Model 56 pack	(Italy)
	105 mm M101	(USA)
	Hawk SAM	(USA)
Anti-tank	Dragon ATGW	(USA)
Mortars	81 mm M29	(USA)
	81 mm L16A1	(UK)
Infantry	Designs from Austria, West Germany, Italy and USA	

Saudi Arabia is the only user of the AMX-30 DCA twin 30 mm anti-aircraft tank. (C. Foss)

SENEGAL

Strength: 7500
Gendarmerie 1600
Military service: Two years selective conscription
Background: An ex-French colony, Senegal follows most of the other small African states in being poor and undeveloped. The small army represents the main source of stability in the country but so far there have been no serious internal difficulties and the frontiers have not been threatened. Training is overseen by a small French mission and the capability of the army is probably better than many of its neighbours.
Structure: The country is divided into four military districts with the concentration of troops at the capital Dakar and along the northern border where there is fear of infiltration by the Polisario who are operating in the desert.
4 infantry battalions
1 engineer battalion
1 reconnaissance squadron
2 'parachute' companies
2 'commando' companies
1 artillery battery

Equipment: All weapons and equipment are imported, largely from France.

AFVs

Armoured cars	Panhard M-3, M-8	(France)	} 12
	AML-60/90	(France)	
APCs	VXB-170	(France)	12
Artillery	105 mm M101		
	howitzer	(USA)	6
	30 mm, 40 mm LAA	(France)	
Mortars	81 mm	(France)	
Infantry	All of French origin		

SIERRA LEONE

Strength: 2800
900 police
Military service: Voluntary
Background: The army is supposed to consist of two infantry battalions with supporting arms but it seems more likely that it is the elements of two battalions and may even be a number of independent infantry companies. The state of training and general military capability is probably low and the troops would in general be used only to support the police in the event of a breakdown of law and order. Equipment is elderly with an unknown state of readiness and consists of 10 MOWAG armoured cars and some 60 mm and 81 mm mortars.

SINGAPORE

Strength: 30 000
Reserves, 45 000
Military service: Two+ years
Background: The role of the army is the defence of the frontiers, the maintenance of internal security and youth training. But there is a more subtle role in that the presence of this well-trained and effective force demonstrates to the world, and particularly the Far Eastern commercial world, that Singapore is a stable and properly organised city state which will stand no nonsense from troublesome elements, and is therefore a safe and reliable place in which to invest. Above all, Singapore relies on foreign investment and trade and it is believed that an efficient defence force is worth the considerable expense it costs. Another aspect is that the force, and particularly the army, welds together the disparate nationalities in the Singapore population, and to do this the pattern of the Israeli army has been deliberately copied. Israeli teams oversee most of the military training and efficiency is high. All troops serve at home in the Singapore islands, but some fought in the Borneo confrontation of the mid-1960s.

Cadillac Gage V-200 Commandos of the Singapore Army on parade.

SINGAPORE

Structure: The regular units can be rapidly reinforced with the TA, which is a well-trained and formed body. There is one divisional HQ which looks likely to be swamped with units on mobilisation, but the sort of defensive operations that are likely to occur would probably be fought with brigade actions.

1 divisional HQ
1 armoured brigade HQ
1 tank battalion
2 mechanised infantry battalions
3 infantry brigade HQ
9 infantry battalions
3 artillery battalions
2 engineer battalions
3 signals battalions

Equipment: There is an arms factory in Singapore and it is expanding its capability, but most equipment is imported.

AFVs Tanks	AMX-13 light	(France)	75
APCs	M113	(USA)	250
	V-150/V-200 Commando	(USA)	280
Artillery	155 mm M68 towed gun	(Israel)	
Anti-tank	106 mm M40A1 RCL	(USA)	
Mortars	120 mm	(Singapore)	
Infantry	Some UK products. M16 rifles made in Singapore under licence and some Australian L1A1 rifles.		

SOMALIA

Strength: 45 000
Militia, 20 000
Military service: Voluntary
Background: The state of the army is unclear, since the recent war with Ethiopia has left the Somalis in disarray. The figures quoted in this report should be treated with some reserve since they cannot be checked, but it is apparent that the army is both large and poorly-equipped. Training is poor and the performance of some units in the war was bad. Experienced leadership is lacking and since the Soviets are now concentrating their attentions on Ethiopia, Somalia is in dire need of a sponsor to guide her.
Structure: It should not be assumed that the formations and units are in any way up to strength and it could easily be that some of them do not exist at all.

  7 divisional HQ
  2 tank brigades
 20 infantry brigades
  1 'commando' brigade
 13 artillery regiments
 10 AA regiments

Equipment: All equipment is imported and most of it is in a poor state of repair.

AFVs	Tanks	T-34	(USSR)	50
		T-54/55	(USSR)	30
Scout cars		BRDM-2	(USSR)	
APCs		BTR-40/50/60	(USSR)	50
		BTR-152	(USSR)	100
		*V-150 Commando	(USA)	} a few
		*M113	(USA)	
		FIAT 6614	(Italy)	
Artillery		130 mm M46	(USSR)	
		122 mm M1931/1938	(USSR)	
		100 mm M1944/1955	(USSR)	180 approx
		85 mm D-44	(USSR)	
		76 mm M1942	(USSR)	
		23 mm ZSU-23-4 LAA	(USSR)	
		SA-2/3 SAM	(USSR)	
Anti-tank		100 mm	(USSR)	
		*106 mm M40A1 RCL	(USA)	
		*MILAN ATGW	(France)	

Items marked * may have been supplied by Saudi Arabia

SOUTH AFRICA

Strength: 48 500 (40 000 conscripts)
Reserves, approximately 360 000 available
Military service: Two years
Background: The South African Army has the two difficult tasks of safeguarding the long frontiers (particularly the troublesome northern one) and maintaining peace inside the country. Both have strained it to near the limit in the last ten years. Rather like New Zealand, South Africa depends upon a small regular force which can be rapidly expanded to four or five times its peacetime size in an emergency. It has been said that there could be more than 250,000 whites under arms in a matter of days. The regular element inevitably spends much effort in training the conscripts who, after their service go to the part-time Citizen Force and this is the mainstay of the army even though it only exists in cadre form until mobilisation is declared. In the last few years there have been indications that morale and motivation among both regulars and conscripts has suffered and dropped but the basic toughness of the South African is unlikely to have changed so quickly and it must be assumed that the army would always fight doggedly and skilfully in defence of the Homeland.

Structure: The Citizen Force is organised as a corps comprising two divisions each with a number of brigades. The

South African infantry on assault course. (South African Army/MARS)

HQ are manned by regulars and are sited in the towns and cities with the various units centred in the surrounding countryside.
1 corps HQ
2 divisional HQ (1 armoured, 1 infantry)
1 parachute brigade
1 SAM regiment (Cactus)
The following exist in cadre form:
1 armoured brigade
2 mechanised brigades
4 motorised brigades
13 artillery regiments
9 LAA regiments
10 engineer squadrons
5 signals regiments

Equipment: There is an active arms industry and a large proportion of the army's needs are met by the national factories, particularly the light weapons and ammunition. For the remainder, spares are bought when and where they can be found, and the state of readiness is apparently remarkably high.

AFVs Tanks	Centurion	(UK)		250
				approx
	Comet	(UK)		20
Armoured cars	Eland (AML-90)	(South Africa)		1600
Scout cars	Ferret	(UK)		
	T17E1 Staghound	(USA)	}	230

APCs	Ratel 20	(South Africa)		1000
	Saracen	(UK)		280
	Hippo, Rhino	(South Africa)		500
				approx
SP guns	25 pdr Sexton	(Canada)		50
	105 mm M7	(USA)		
Artillery	155 mm gun	(Israel, perhaps)		
	5.5 in medium gun	(UK)		15
	25 pdr	(UK)		125
	3.7in medium AA	(UK)		
	40 mm Bofors L/70 LAA	(Sweden)		
	35 mm GDF-001 LAA	(Switzerland)		
	Cactus (Crotale) SAM	(France)		18
	Tigercat SAM	(UK)		
Anti-tank	90 mm gun			
	17 pdr gun	(UK)		15
Mortars	120 mm, 81 mm	(Israel)		200
Infantry				

Practically all are manufactured in South Africa from licenced designs provided by Belgium and Israel. There are many elderly UK weapons still in service and a few home designs

SPAIN

Strength: 200 000 (150 000 conscripts)
Reserves, approximately 500 000
Military service: 16 months
Background: The army has a long and honourable tradition, broken only by the Civil War. It has the usual role of safeguarding the nation and maintaining peace, but the real responsibility for internal security rests with the police and Civil Guard and the army would only be called in for a desperate emergency. During the last 40 years it has acted as a useful stabilising influence on the youth of the nation by making all mix together in their conscript service. It is now being slowly re-equipped and finding a new role in which it is to be hoped that it can cooperate with its European partners to a greater extent. The state of training and operational readiness is probably much lower than in comparable armies in Europe, but the manpower is traditionally tough. Great reliance is placed on the Territorial Defence Forces who would defend the national boundaries while the regular formations could be manoeuvred anywhere as an intervention force.
Structure: The army is divided into the Intervention Force, which is predominantly regular, and the Territorial Defence Forces which rely to some extent on reservists to bring them up to strength but which nevertherless contain such elements as the mountain troops. There is also the Spanish Foreign Legion which is entirely regular. In addition there are some specialised troops such as the missile battalions which are not in any divisional formation but are kept directly under command of the Commander-in-Chief.

Intervention Forces
  1 armoured division
  1 mechanised division
  1 motorised infantry division
  1 armoured cavalry brigade
  1 parachute brigade
  1 airportable brigade
Territorial Defence Forces
  2 armoured cavalry brigades
  1 light cavalry regiment
  1 mountain brigade
10 independent infantry brigades
  2 artillery brigades
Foreign Legion
  3 Foreign Legion regiments
  4 infantry groups
Army Units
12 artillery regiments
  7 engineer regiments
  2 signals regiments
  2 commando companies
  2 special forces companies
  1 SAM battalion (Nike Hercules, Hawk)

Equipment: Spain has a flourishing arms industry, though it is mainly inclined to the lighter end of the spectrum. Heavier items have been largely obtained through US off-shore programmes.

AFVs Tanks	AMX-30	(France)	200
	M47	(USA)	340
	M48	(USA)	110
	M41 light	(USA)	180
Armoured cars	AML-60	(France)	90
	AML-90	(France)	100
APCs	BMR-600	(Spain)	
	M113	(USA)	540
SP guns	105 mm M108	(USA)	48
	155 mm M44	(USA)	10
	155 mm M109	(USA)	70
	175 mm M107	(USA)	10
	203 mm M110	(USA)	4

Artillery	203 mm M115	(USA)	
	155 mm M114	(USA)	
	105 mm Model 56 pack	(Italy)	
	105 mm M101	(USA)	
	105 mm m/26	(Spain)	850
	300 mm D10 RL	(Spain)	
	216 mm E21 RL	(Spain)	
	108 mm E20/32 RL	(Spain)	
	90 mm M117 AA	(USA)	150
	40 mm Bofors L/70 LAA	(Sweden)	
	20 mm, 35 mm LAA	(Switzerland)	
	Nike Hercules SAM	(USA)	
	Improved Hawk SAM	(USA)	
Anti-tank	106 mm M40A1 RCL	(USA)	
	SS11 ATGW	(France)	
	MILAN ATGW	(France)	
	Dragon ATGW	(USA)	
	Cobra ATGW	(West Germany)	
Mortars	81 mm, 120 mm	(Spain)	
Infantry	Designed and manufactured in Spain		

177

SRI LANKA

Strength: 8900
Reserves, 9000
Military service: Voluntary
Background: The principal role of the small army is to provide support for the police in the event of a total breakdown of law and order. Fortunately this seems remote, the island is peaceful and is a neutral with no external commitments. The army closely resembles the Indian Army in its regimental system and place in the community. Training is good and is centralised.
Structure: Both the regular and the reserve force are organised in regiments much like British ones; there are brigades, but it is thought that units generally act on their own.

1 brigade HQ
1 reconnaissance regiment
3 infantry battalions
1 artillery regiment
1 engineer regiment
1 signals regiment

Equipment: There is no arms industry and almost all weapons and equipment are elderly and well worn. Maintenance is good. Practically all the infantry weapons are British.

AFVs

Armoured cars	Saladin	(UK)	6
Scout cars	Ferret	(UK)	30
APCs	BTR-152	(USSR)	10
Artillery	85 mm D-44	(USSR)	
	76 mm M48 mountain gun	(Yugoslavia)	

SUDAN

Strength: 60 000
Reserves, 3500 para-military forces

Background: Until 1976 the army was predominantly infantry and a counter-insurgency and internal security force. Since then there has been a steady alteration in its make-up to turn it into more of a conventional army capable of offering a viable defence of the country's long frontiers. Operational experience is limited to counter-insurgency but training is good and the troops, while relatively unsophisticated in outlook, are tough, resilient and intelligent.

Structure: The structure of the army is based on the British, from which it is descended. The operational formation is the brigade, and this is an independent formation composed of all arms. There is a divisional structure, but this is more for administration than for operational use.

2 armoured brigades
7 infantry brigades
1 parachute brigade
3 artillery regiments
3 AA regiments
1 engineer regiment

Equipment: Until the early 1970s all equipment came from the Eastern Bloc. Since then there has been a change of heart and purchases are now being made from the West. The result is a mixture of equipment of all ages. There are now some modern US AFVs on order.

AFVs Tanks	T-54/55	(USSR)	130
	T-62 light	(PRC)	30
Armoured cars	Saladin	(UK)	50
	Ferret	(UK)	50
APCs	BTR-40/50/60	(USSR)	100
	V-150 Commando	(USA)	45
	OT-64	(Czechoslovakia)	60
	AMX-10P	(France)	50
Artillery	122 mm M1938	(USSR)	18
	105 mm M101	(USA)	20
	100 mm M1944	(USSR)	40
	25 pdr	(UK)	55
	37 mm, 40 mm LAA	(USSR/Sweden)	150
Anti-tank	85 mm M1945	(USSR)	30
Mortars	120 mm M1943	(USSR)	30
Infantry	Most weapons of West German origin		

SWEDEN

Strength: 45 000 (36 000 conscripts)
Reserves, approximately 750 000 on mobilisation
Military service: 8 months–15 months depending on rank and ability
Background: Sweden is neutral and the purpose of the army is to maintain that neutrality as well as making contributions to UN forces. Conscripts are trained in special training regiments and serve for a time dependent upon their military task and rank. Refresher training for reservists is carefully carried out and the intention is that practically every able-bodied man in the country could be turned out to defend it if there was an invasion. The regular personnel are well trained in central schools and academies but for more than 100 years the army has had no operational experience apart from UN peacekeeping activities.

Structure: The entire thinking of the army is defensive in character and the largest operational formation is the brigade. There are three-types, armoured, infantry and Norrland. The latter is essentially a lightly-armed infantry brigade with semi-arctic equipment.

Peace establishment
  47 training regiments
    UNFICYP battalion (Cyprus)
    UNEF battalion (Egypt)
War establishment
  5 armoured brigades
  20 infantry brigades
  4 Norrland brigades
  50 independent infantry, artillery and AA battalions
 100 independent Local Defence battalions
 400+ Local Defence companies

Bandvagn Bv206 all-terrain vehicle of the Swedish Army.
(C. Foss)

Equipment: There is a flourishing and competent arms industry with a large export trade. About 10% of all equipment is bought abroad, the rest is manufactured in Sweden.

AFVs Tanks

	Strv 101	(Sweden)	} 350
	Strv 102 (Centurion)	(UK)	
	Strv 103 (S Tank)	(Sweden)	} 310
	Ikv 91 light	(Sweden)	
APCs	Pbv 302A	(Sweden)	
SP guns	155 mm Bk 1A	(Sweden)	

Artillery	155 mm FH-77	(Sweden)
	150 mm m/39	(Sweden)
	105 mm Type 4140	(Sweden)
	57 mm m/54 Bofors LAA	(Sweden)
	40 mm m/36, L/70 Bofors LAA	(Sweden)
	RBS-70 SAM	(Sweden)
	Redeye SAM	(USA)
	Hawk SAM	(USA)
Anti-tank	90 mm RCL	(Sweden)
	84 mm Carl Gustaf RCL	(Sweden)
	Bantam ATGW	(Sweden)
Mortars	120 mm m/41	(Finland/Sweden)
Infantry	Mixture of native designs and licence-built foreign ones, all made in Sweden. Most have minor adaptions to suit the climatic conditions	

Swedish infantry on manoeuvres armed with Carl Gustaf RCLs and 9 mm model 45 SMGs. (I. V. Hogg)

183

SWITZERLAND

Strength: 18 500 (15 000 conscripts)
Reserves, approximately 600 000
Military service: 17 weeks recruit training + refreshers annually
Background: The role of the army is to preserve the neutrality of the country and it is wholly defensive in character. Recruitment is unusual in that the very small standing army merely provides a cadre of training leaders and a few high-ranking wartime officers. Every able-bodied man in the nation is required to undergo military service and remains liable for call-out until aged 50. Units have close territorial links and on call-out men report to a nearby location, with their personal weapons which they keep at home. Refresher training is conscientiously carried out and there is no doubt that the Swiss could put up a most spirited defence if they were invaded.
Structure: The four corps control specific territorial areas with 3 Corps based on a main mountain keep which would become the final defensive position. There are Border Brigades which would fight delaying action from the frontiers backwards, while other brigades provide support facilities and local defence within the corps areas.
War Strength
 4 corps HQ
 3 armoured divisions
 6 infantry divisions
 3 mountain divisions

23 independent infantry brigades
 1 armoured car battalion, 3 heavy artillery regiments
 2 engineer regiments, 2 signals regiments
Equipment: There is an active and competent arms industry, though many large items are imported. The policy is to be as independent of foreign supply as is possible, yet to go to competitive tender on the open market. Maintenance is extremely good and all equipment is at a high state of readiness.

AFVs	Tanks	Centurion	(UK)	320
		AMX-13	(France)	
		Pz-61	(Switzerland)	150
		Pz-68	(Switzerland)	370
	APCs	M113	(USA)	1250
	SP guns	155 mm M109	(USA)	260
Artillery		105 mm Model 35	(Switzerland)	
		105 mm Model 46	(Switzerland)	
		40 mm Bofors L/70 LAA	(Sweden)	
		20 mm, 35 mm LAA	(Switzerland)	
Anti-tank		90 mm Model 50/57 gun	(Switzerland)	
		106 mm M40A1 RCL	(USA)	
		Bantam ATGW	(Switzerland)	
Mortars		81 mm, 120 mm	(Switzerland)	
Infantry		All weapons Swiss in design and manufacture		

SYRIA

Strength: 200 000
Reserves, approximately 100 000
Military service: 30 months
Background: The overwhelming reason for the large army is the part it plays in the Arab-Israeli conflict, however it now deploys about 30 000 men in Lebanon. The maintenance of this disproportionately large army is a heavy burden on the country and there is a good deal of political activity in which the army is involved. In fact the secondary reason for the army is to carry out government policy in the country. Training is probably as good as in any other Middle Eastern conscript army, but it is not likely that the reserves are organised or that any practical refresher training is carried out.

Structure: There does not appear to be a corps HQ to control the several divisions and it seems likely that when the entire army is deployed, as happened in the 1973 war, each division acts more or less independently on orders from the Army commander. This arrangement limits the flexibility of the field force considerably.

2 armoured divisions (Soviet type)
3 mechanised divisions (Soviet type)
4 independent armoured brigades
1 independent mechanised brigade
4 infantry brigades
2 artillery brigades
6 'commando' battalions
4 parachute battalions (airlift for only 1)
1 SSM battalion (Frog, Scud)
48 SAM batteries (SA-2/3/6)

Equipment: The great majority of the equipment is Soviet in origin and Syria is aware of the dangers of mixing West and East weaponry; however, she has used her oil money to buy some items from the West which are superior to Soviet equivalents.

AFVs	Tanks	T-34	(USSR)	200
		T-54/55	(USSR)	1500
		T-62	(USSR)	900
		T-72	(USSR)	
		PT-76 light	(USSR)	100

Scout cars	BRDM 1/2	(USSR)	
APCs	BMP	(USSR)	
	BTR-40/50/60/152	(USSR)	1600
	OT-64	(Czechoslovakia)	
SP guns	152 mm ISU-152	(USSR)	
	122 mm ISU-122	(USSR)	
Artillery	180 mm S-23	(USSR)	
	152 mm M1937/D-1	(USSR)	
	130 mm M-46	(USSR)	800
	122 mm M1931/ 38/D-30	(USSR)	
	85 mm D-44	(USSR)	
	140 mm BM-14 RL	(USSR)	
	122 mm BM-21 RL	(USSR)	
	Frog 7 SSM	(USSR)	30
	Scud SSM	(USSR)	36
	100 mm KS-19 AA	(USSR)	
	85 mm KS-12 AA	(USSR)	

	23 mm, 37 mm, 57 mm LAA guns	(USSR)	
	57 mm ZSU-57-2 LAA	(USSR)	
	23 mm ZSU-23-4 LAA	(USSR)	
	SA-7/9 SAM	(USSR)	
Anti-tank	57 mm, 85 mm, 100 mm towed guns	(USSR)	
	Snapper ATGW	(USSR)	
	Sagger ATGW	(USSR)	
	MILAN ATGW	(France)	(on order)
Mortars	160 mm M43	(USSR)	
	120 mm M1943	(USSR)	
Infantry	All weapons either Soviet or Czechoslovak manufactured		

TAIWAN

Strength: 320 000
Reserves, 100 000
Military service: Two years
Background: The Republic of China on Taiwan is an isolated nation and the proper role of its large army is unclear. During the lifetime of Chian Kai-shek it was always said that the Republic would invade the mainland and reinstate its previous form of government. This is obviously impracticable since the PLA would defeat any such attempt in a very short time. The only justification for retaining such a disproportionately large force must be a fear for national security should the USA withdraw its shielding naval forces. One quarter of the army is based on Quemoy and Matsu, two small off-shore islands within artillery range of the mainland. There are regular exchanges of fire, but little else and the army has had no war experience since it left the mainland in 1949. Training is thorough and detailed. All reservists are given regular refresher training, all of which is on the American model.
Structure: The army is a close copy of the United States model.
Equipment: Taiwan produces about two-thirds of its military needs, but artillery and armoured vehicles are imported from the USA. Everything is of US origin or pattern and the scale of issue is almost lavish.

AFVs	Tanks	M41 light	(USA)	650
		M47/48 medium	(USA)	180
	APCs	M113	(USA)	1100
	SP guns	105 mm M108	(USA)	225
		76 mm M18	(USA)	150
Artillery		203 mm M55	(USA)	90
		155 mm M59	(USA)	} 300
		155 mm M114	(USA)	
		105 mm M101	(USA)	550
		75 mm M116 pack	(USA)	350
		Honest John SSM	(USA)	
		Hsiung Fen SSM	(Taiwan)	
		126 mm Kung Feng RL	(Taiwan)	
		Hawk SAM	(USA)	
		Nike Hercules SAM	(USA)	
		Chaparral SAM	(USA)	20
		40 mm L/60 gun AA	(Sweden/USA)	300
Anti-tank		106 mm M40A1 RCL	(USA)	500
		TOW ATGW	(USA)	
Mortars		81 mm	(USA)	
Infantry		All other infantry weapons are entirely US in origin or made under licence		

TANZANIA

Strength: 50 000
Para-military forces, approximately 3500
Military service: Voluntary
Background: The army has deliberately not followed the British example which was inherited on independence in 1964 and has modelled itself on rather looser lines. The results have not always been happy, and though the army was welcome in Uganda when Amin was being thrown out, discipline does not always seem to have been a strong point in its favour. The army is now withdrawing back to Tanzania (May 1981) and when it is within its national borders the necessity for such a large and expensive force will have to be reconsidered.
Structure: Broadly speaking, organisation and training have been on communist lines, with Chinese and Cuban advisers. Within the limits of the equipment available the army is structured more or less as if it were a Soviet satellite, but it is predominantly an infantry force. It probably operates at unit level and the higher formations may be more administrative than operational.
1 divisional HQ
9 infantry brigades
1 tank regiment
9 artillery battalions
1 engineer regiment

Equipment: As far as was possible equipment came from China, however other Warsaw Pact items were obtained as well, so there is some mixing of types.

AFVs Tanks	T-59	(PRC)	20
	T-60	(PRC)	
	T-62	(USSR)	20
APCs	BTR-40/152	(USSR)	
	K-63	(PRC)	
Artillery	122 mm M1931	(USSR)	
	76 mm M1942	(USSR)	
	37 mm LAA	(USSR)	
	SA-3/6 SAM	(USSR)	
Mortars	120 mm M43	(USSR)	
Infantry	Mixture of Soviet and Chinese of all ages		

THAILAND

Strength: 145 000
Reserves, up to 500 000
Military service: Two years
Background: The army has played a part in the political life
of the country for the past 50 years. The major role of the
army has therefore been as an instrument of government,
if not the actual government itself. The second role is
counter-insurgency and in this the army has had much
practice. There are four military districts in the country and
it seems that formations in each district are broken down
into units and spread around the region. There is a con-
tinuous internal security campaign being waged, particularly along the Cambodian and north-eastern borders.
Structure: The army is modelled on that of the USA 20
years ago. The general standard of training and ability is
high and the army is well able to hold the frontiers and
repel a moderate invasion. It is not well organised to
launch aggressive operations and lacks much of the supporting services which would be needed for that, but a
division was maintained in Viet-Nam.
1 cavalry division
6 infantry divisions
3 independent combat teams
4 parachute and special forces battalions
1 SAM battalion (Hawk)
5 aviation companies

Equipment: Equipment is US in origin, almost without
exception. There is a small arms industry which is just
developing.

AFVs Tanks		M48 medium	(USA)	20
		M41 light	(USA)	150
Armoured cars		Shorland	(UK)	32
APCs		M113	(USA)	250
		LVTP-7	(USA)	40
		V-150 Commando	(USA)	20
		Saracen	(UK)	20
Artillery		155 mm M114	(USA)	50
		105 mm M101	(USA)	300
		40 mm Bofors LAA	(USA/Sweden)	40
		Hawk SAM	(USA)	40
Anti-tank		106 mm M40A1 RCL	(USA)	
Infantry		US in origin		

TOGO

Strength: 3000
Military service: Two years, selective conscription
Background: The army is too small to be an effective defence against any incursion and it really exists to ensure internal security and to uphold government.

Structure
2 infantry battalions
2 motorised battalions
1 'commando' company
1 engineer company

Equipment

AFVs

Armoured cars	M8	(USA)	} 8
	AML Panhard	(France)	
APCs	M3	(USA)	} 5
	UR-416	(West Germany)	
Infantry	Mixture of French and West German weapons		

TUNISIA

Strength: 18 000 (12 000 conscripts)
Para-military forces, 6000
Military service: 12 months selective conscription
Background: The army has the triple roles of defending the nation, ensuring internal security and taking part in civil projects. In fact the first role is not easily foreseeable with the present military structure since the best that the army could do would be to hinder and delay any incursion. The main effort in equipment and training seems to be directed towards the latter two roles. The army largely depends on the core of 6000 regulars and the one year conscription is not long enough to do more than impart the necessary training.
Structure: The organisation is based on the French model and there is no real operational formation higher than the individual unit.
2 combined arms regiments
1 Sahara regiment
1 para-commando battalion
1 artillery battalion
1 engineer battalion

Equipment: The two main sources of equipment are France and the USA, but odd items have been bought from other countries, which probably does not help maintenance.

AFVs Tanks	AMX-13	(France)	30
	M41 light	(USA)	20
Armoured cars	EBR-75	(France)	15
	Saladin	(UK)	20
	M113	(USA)	on order
SP guns	90 mm		
	Jagdpanzer K	(Austria)	45
Artillery	155 mm M114	(USA)	10
	105 mm M101	(USA)	40
	40 mm Bofors		
	L/70 LAA	(Sweden)	
Anti-tank	SS11 ATGW	(France)	
	TOW ATGW	(USA)	on order
Infantry	Mixture of Austrian, British and Italian weapons		

Tunisia uses the British Mk 4 Sterling SMG. (C. Foss)

TURKEY

Strength: 470 000 (200 000 conscripts)
Reserves, approximately 400 000
Military service: 20 months
Background: The army is organised for home defence and does not have a role in internal security except when martial law is declared. It is a predominantly infantry force and forms the southern anchor of the NATO alliance. It, like Norway, has a common border with the USSR and this fact has a marked effect on the deployment of the formations. There is also a continual friction with Greece, culminating in the invasion of Cyprus in 1974 and this will take time to heal. The army is well trained and the toughness of the Turkish soldier is a well-known fact. The reserves are a rather different matter since it seems that there is no organised refresher training for them, but they are liable for recall until 46 years old.
Structure: There are four Army commands each with two or three corps. One command has the responsibility for the Soviet border while the one with the bulk of the armour is based on Istanbul and would carry out the function of a large mobile reserve. Many of the formations are below strength and would need the recall of the reserve to come up to war establishment.

1 armoured division
2 mechanised infantry divisions
14 infantry divisions
5 armoured brigades
4 mechanised infantry brigades
5 independent infantry brigades
1 parachute brigade
1 commando brigade
4 SSM battalions (Honest John)

Equipment: There is a growing arms industry, largely government-owned and financed. Much of the equipment is elderly, which is slowly being put right, and almost all of it is American in origin. Orders are outstanding for Leopard 1 tanks and TOW and MILAN ATGW.

AFVs	Tanks	M47/48	(USA)	3500
		M60	(USA)	
	APCs	M113	(USA)	
		M59	(USA)	1600
		V-150 Commando	(USA)	
		M3 Half-track	(USA)	
	SP guns	203 mm M110	(USA)	
		175 mm M107	(USA)	36
		155 mm M44/ M109		190
		105 mm M7/ M108	(USA)	265

UGANDA

Artillery	203 mm M115	(USA)	
	155 mm M59/		
	M114	(USA)	
	105 mm M101	(USA)	1500
	75 mm M116		
	pack	(USA)	
	Honest John SSM	(USA)	18
	40 mm M1 LAA	(USA/Sweden)	900
Anti-tank	106 mm M40A1		
	RCL	(USA)	800
	57 mm, 75 mm		
	RCL	(USA)	1600
	Cobra ATGW	(West Germany)	85
	SS11 ATGW	(France)	
	TOW ATGW	(USA)	Some
Mortars	81 mm, 4.2 in	(USA)	1000
Infantry	Large proportion of US models, with licence-made West German rifles and some native designs of other weapons		

Background: It is not possible to give an accurate idea of the Ugandan army at the time of writing since it disintegrated in the face of the Tanzanian invasion of the country and is only slowly being built up again. Before the invasion it was about 20,000 men armed with the usual selection of Soviet weapons and equipment but it was quickly proved that the effects of the Amin administration had been to destroy the morale of the men and the readiness of the equipment. How much can be salvaged from the remains has yet to be determined, but it would seem likely and indeed fairly sensible for the Tanzanians to take what they need of the weapons and leave Uganda to start afresh.

UNION OF SOVIET SOCIALIST REPUBLICS

Strength: 1 825 000
Reserves, approximately 4 000 000 are probably available
Para-military forces: 200 000 Border Troops. 250 000 Security Troops
Military service: Two years
Background: The sheer size of the Soviet Army makes it difficult to describe in a few words. Although there are 170+ divisions in the active army it is important to recall that they all have three levels of readiness. Level 1 is at 75-100% strength and is fully equipped. Level 2 is at 50-75% strength, but equipped. Level 3 is only about 33% strong, though equipped. In Eastern Europe and in the WP countries the divisions are at Level 1, but inside the USSR and for some divisions on the Far Eastern border areas the strength is Level 2 or 3. Such a huge war machine is inevitably strongly centralised in its command structure and this is probably its greatest weakness. However, there is no doubt that the state of training of the units is good to very good and though much equipment is strong and unsophisticated even now, it is above all reliable and effective.

The army has four roles; defence of the Homeland is an obvious one, and it must be remembered that Russia has been invaded many times and the German incursions of 1941-45 are well remembered. Secondly, the army has the role of deterring attack, especially nuclear attack. Thirdly it has the role of supporting communist rule in the satellite countries and finally, of projecting Soviet political manoeuvres throughout the world. It will be noticed that internal security does not enter into the picture since that is the responsibility of the Security forces. No training is given in counter-insurgency in the way that such training is understood in the West.

Whether or not morale and motivation are high in the Soviet Army depends upon the degree of wishfulness in the reader's mind, but at all events it can be asserted that the army will fight effectively and aggressively whenever it is employed. The enormous pool of reserve manpower is given sufficient training to ensure that when recalled, the men are able to take their place in their units.

Soviet infantry in the assault during winter exercises. Leading man is carrying RPG-7 anti-tank weapon. (I. V. Hogg)

Structure: The highest Soviet Army organisation is a Front, which would only be formed in war. A Front comprises several Armies and an Army corresponds to a Western Corps. There are several Soviet armies in Eastern Europe, forming the equivalent of military districts. A speciality of the Soviet Army is that it can form specific tank armies built up from tank and mechanised divisions. The majority of the Soviet Army is in Eastern Russia, west of the Urals and close enough to the border with the West to be able to reinforce that area with the minimum delay. However, many of these divisions are at Level 2 and 3, so that there has to be a lapse of time and some hurried activity before they could be considered operational. Nevertheless, the numbers of men and armoured vehicles that could be moved towards Western Europe is formidable, and the Army figures do not include the large force which holds and operates the nuclear weapons of the USSR.

Although the Chinese threat and the several activities along the Afghan and Iranian borders will have caused some diversion of effort from Europe, the numbers available to the Soviet High Command are so large that the alterations in force level directed at NATO are unlikely to be noticeable just yet.

 46 tank divisions
118 motor rifle divisions
  8 airborne divisions

Deployment

Eastern Europe
  East Germany
   10 tank divisions
   10 motor rifle divisions
  Poland
   2 motor rifle divisions
  Hungary
   2 tank divisions
   2 motor rifle divisions
Czechoslovakia
   2 tank divisions
   3 motor rifle divisions
European USSR
  23 (approx) tank divisions
  29 motor rifle divisions
   8 airborne divisions
Central USSR
   1 tank division
   5 motor rifle divisions
Southern USSR
   1 tank division
  23 motor rifle divisions
Chinese border
   6 tank divisions
  43 motor rifle divisions

Equipment: There is a huge arms industry which is allotted a high priority by the government. A feature of Soviet design thinking is to continually improve on existing products and to be cautious at introducing radically new systems. The result is that there are quite large families of equipments, such as the medium tanks, in which the later models still retain many of the features of the early ones, but are more sophisticated and effective while not requiring much alteration in the training arrangements for the crew or in maintenance procedures. It is fashionable to assert that Soviet equipment is cruder and less effective than that of the western nations, but this is rapidly becoming less and less true. The output of the Soviet factories is prodigious and they are able to supply an astonishing number of satellite and client countries with complete armouries of weapons and vehicles. This same high output enables them to build enough of one weapon for the Soviet Army to change over to it in a very short time—much less than that needed by western countries who are more exposed to market forces and low government funding.

AFVs Tanks	IS-2/3/4		
	T-10		
	T-34		
	T-54/55/62/64	(USSR)	50 000
	T-72		
	PT-76		
Reconnaissance and scout cars	BMP-R		
	BRDM-1		
	BRDM-2		
APCs	BTR-40/50/60		
	BTR-152	(USSR)	55 000
	BMP-1		
	ATP		
	MTLB		
SP guns	152 mm ISU-152		
	122 mm ISU-122		
	100 mm SU-100	(USSR)	10 800
	85 mm ASU-85		
	57 mm ASU-57		

Soviet tank men prepare for an exercise. (I. V. Hogg)

UNION OF SOVIET SOCIALIST REPUBLICS

Artillery			
180 mm S-23			
152 mm D-1/D-20			
130 mm SM-4-1/ M46	(USSR)	20 000	
122 mm D-30/ M1938			
85 mm SD-44			
76 mm mountain			
250 mm BM-25 RL			
240 mm BM-24 RL			
140 mm RPU-14/ BM-14-17 RL	(USSR)	7200	
122 mm BM-21 RL			
Frog SSM			
SS-21 SSM	(USSR)	1300	
Scud SSM			
SS-12 Scaleboard SSM			
23 mm, 57 mm LAA			
ZSU-23-4 LAA	(USSR)	9000	
ZSU-57-2 LAA			

SA-4 Ganef SAM			
SA-6 Gainful SAM			
SA-7 Grail SAM	(USSR)		
SA-8 Gecko SAM			
SA-9 Gaskin SAM			
SA-11 SAM			
Anti-tank	100 mm T-12 gun	(USSR)	
	73 mm SPG-9 RCL		
	Snapper ATGW		
	Swatter ATGW		
	Sagger ATGW	(USSR)	8000
	Spigot ATGW		
	Spandrel ATGW		
	Spiral ATGW		
Mortars	240 mm M240		
	160 mm M60		
	120 mm M43	(USSR)	7,200
	107 mm M107		
	82 mm M37		
Infantry	AK-74 rifles		
	AKM rifles		
	RPK, PK MG		
	RPG-7 ATk RL		

UNITED ARAB EMIRATES

Strength: 23 000
Reserves, no formed reserves
Military service: Voluntary, with conscription in addition
Background: Military service is not attractive in the oil-rich
kingdoms of the UAE and the conscription law is intended
to back-up when recruiting is unsatisfactory. So far it does
not seem to have been invoked. The armed forces probably have the main role of internal security and with this is
prestige, since the area is one which respects armed force.
It is most unlikely that the small army could hold off an
attack for more than a day or two. Only a proportion of the
manpower is native to the area, many being recruited from
other Middle East countries. Training is generally good,
though greatly dependent upon outside assistance.
Structure: The general pattern of the army is based on the
British, where many of the officers and men were trained.
There are three regional commands, Abu Dhabi, Dhubai
and Ras al-Khaima. For the most part the troops are
stationed out in the country in small units and sub-units,
often based on stone forts.
1 Royal Guard Brigade (approximately a large battalion)
4 armoured car battalions
7 infantry battalions
3 artillery battalions
3 AA battalions

Equipment: There is no arms industry, but the UAE hope
to benefit from the proposed AIO and have contributed
money to it. Most equipment is British, with some French
and a little American also.

AFVs

Reconnaissance vehicles	Scorpion	(UK)	30
Armoured cars	Saladin	(UK)	70
	Shorland	(UK)	6
	AML	(France)	
Scout cars	Ferret	(UK)	60
APCs	AMX-VCI	(France)	
	Panhard M-3	(France)	
	Saracen	(UK)	12
SP guns	155 mm AMX Mk F3	(France)	8
Artillery	105 mm Light Gun	(UK)	
	25 pdr	(UK)	22
	Rapier SAM	(UK)	
	Crotale SAM	(France)	
Anti-tank	120 mm Wombat RCL	(UK)	
	Vigilant ATGW	(UK)	
Mortars	81 mm L16A1	(UK)	
Infantry	Mixture of Belgian, British and West German designs		

UNITED KINGDOM

Strength: 160 000
Reserves, 125 000 regular reserves, 59 000 TA
Military service: Voluntary
Background: The main role of the army is to contribute to the defence of Europe within the framework of NATO. A secondary role is that of Home Defence, including internal security and finally there is a minor responsibility for the peace within the few remaining dependencies and colonies as well as a small contribution to UN peacekeeping. The standard of training is high, though the army has not fought a 'hot' war since Suez in 1956, but there has been plenty of experience in counter-insurgency and there is probably no other army as competent in this role. A disadvantage in the European theatre is the shortage of modern equipment and the lack of money to spend on re-equipping and re-training. Though the army has recently shown that it is both capable and alert and can reinforce West Germany at short notice, there must be concern for the time that it could remain in battle with such limited resources as it now has.

Structure: The army has for generations been organised on a regimental system with officers and men spending the major part of their service life in the same unit. These units are brought together into formations for war, though they are already in them in peacetime. The main operational command is 1st British Corps in West Germany with a separate brigade in West Berlin. Elsewhere in the world there are small forces, some in the remaining dependent territories, and some with UN peacekeeping forces. All others are under the command of United Kingdom Land Forces (UKLF) which is responsible for Home Defence, reinforcement, training and Northern Ireland. There are frequent exercises, both in and out of Europe, which also include the TA. The latter is organised into units and formations and can reinforce quickly, ready for war.

The Chieftain, Main Battle Tank of the British Army.
(C. Foss)

UNITED KINGDOM

1 corps HQ
4 divisional HQ
1 artillery division HQ
10 armoured regiments
9 reconnaissance regiments
48 infantry battalions
5 Gurkha infantry battalions
3 parachute battalions
1 Special Air Service regiment
1 SSM regiment (Lance)
3 AA regiments (Rapier)
18 artillery regiments
9 engineer regiments
6 army aviation regiments
Deployment
United Kingdom
  United Kingdom Mobile Force (UKMF)
    8 Field Force (partly TA)
    7 Field Force (partly TA)
  1 battalion group (ACE Mobile Force)
  1 special air service regiment
  1 Gurkha infantry battalion
  HQ Northern Ireland
    3 infantry brigade HQ
    12-13 infantry battalions
    independent squadrons of engineers, aviation and
signals

West Germany
  BAOR
    1 corps HQ
    4 armoured divisions
    5 Field Force
    1 artillery division
    1 brigade group (West Berlin)
Brunei
  1 Gurkha infantry battalion
Hong Kong
  Gurkha Field Force (3 Gurkha, 1 British battalions)
  Cyprus
  1 infantry battalion (+)
  1 reconnaissance squadron
  1 engineer squadron
  UNFICYP
    1 infantry battalion (−)
    1 reconnaissance squadron
  logistic support
Gibraltar
  1 infantry battalion
  1 engineer squadron
Belize
  1 infantry battalion (−)
  1 reconnaissance troop
  1 artillery battery

1 engineer squadron (−)
logistic support

Equipment: There is a large arms industry with a considerable export trade. Most of the army's weapons and equipment are British made, though the larger artillery pieces are American.

AFVs Tanks	Chieftain	(UK)	900
	Scorpion light	(UK)	270
Armoured cars	Saladin	(UK)	240
	Scimitar (tracked)	(UK)	290
	FV 438 ATGW carrier (tracked)	(UK)	180
Scout cars	Ferret	(UK)	1430
	Fox	(UK)	200
APCs	FV 432	(UK)	2300
	Saracen	(UK)	600
	Spartan	(UK)	60
SP guns	203 mm M110	(USA)	16
	175 mm M107	(USA)	30
	155 mm M109	(USA)	50
	105 mm Abbot	(UK)	155

Artillery	155 mm FH-70	(International)	
	105 mm Model 56 pack	(Italy)	100
	105 mm Light gun	(UK)	
	Lance SSM	(USA)	
	40 mm Bofors L/70 LAA	(UK/Sweden)	
	Blowpipe SAM	(UK)	
	Rapier SAM	(UK)	
Anti-tank	120 mm Wombat RCL	(UK)	
	84 mm Carl Gustaf RCL	(Sweden)	
	Swingfire ATGW	(UK)	
	MILAN ATGW	(France)	
	TOW ATGW	(USA)	on order

Infantry Rifles and MGs variants of Belgian designs. Practically all other weapons British in origin

UNITED STATES OF AMERICA

Strength: 750 800
Reserves, 534 000 (186 000 Army Reserves, 348 000 National Guard)
Military service: Voluntary
Background: The army has survived a very difficult 10 years in which it has all but lost a major war and has changed from a conscript to a volunteer force. It is still wrestling with many problems, not the least being motivation and efficiency, but a major one is manpower. This has led to a number of alterations including the introduction of a substantial proportion of women in non-combatant tasks. The full effects of these changes have yet to be felt, and there must be more still to come. The traditional role of the army has been to fight the major wars of the nation, the smaller wars being the responsibility of the Marine Corps. As a result the Marines have become a sort of surrogate army with considerable military strength (by European standards) and an all-arms structure. The Army has tended in the past to be rather more ponderous and conventional but this is also changing and the necessity to reinforce West Germany rapidly as well as possibly intervene in more distant countries in some strength is making the army more mobile in outlook.

Recruits receive 8 weeks basic training at a large centre and then go to specialist training at another centre before joining a unit and entering its training cycle. The National Guard is organised as a number of operational formations and can be mobilised within a month or 5 weeks to provide the army with more than 8 divisions. The Army Reserve is intended to act as a pool of individual reinforcements.

The army forms the major force in NATO and there is no doubt that it is the chief defence against Soviet aggression anywhere in the world.

M2 Infantry Fighting Vehicle of the US Army. (C. Foss)

Structure: The army has static commitments world-wide as well as a permanent reinforcement role to West Germany and this is reflected in the structure. The division is the main operational formation and there are three types of division, armoured, mechanised and infantry. They differ only in the number and type of units in each and the organisation is purposely flexible so that it can accept more units if it is necessary to bolster its fighting strength. The exception to this rule is the airborne division which is a predominantly infantry force with only light artillery support and no armour.

- 4 armoured divisions
- 5 mechanised infantry divisions
- 5 infantry divisions
- 1 airmobile division
- 1 airborne division
- 1 independent armoured brigade
- 1 independent infantry brigade
- 1 brigade group (West Berlin)
- 3 independent armoured cavalry regiments
- 2 special forces brigades
- 12 SSM battalions

Men of the US 82nd Airborne Division on Exercise Spearpoint, Germany, August 1980. (I. V. Hogg)

Deployment

Continental United States
  Strategic Reserve
    1 mechanised division
    1 airborne division
    1 independent armoured brigade
  Reinforcement for Europe
    2 armoured divisions
    2 mechanised divisions
    3 infantry divisions
    1 airmobile division
    1 independent armoured cavalry regiment
    1 independent infantry brigade
  Alaska
    1 independent infantry brigade
  Panama
    1 independent infantry brigade
Pacific
South Korea
    1 infantry division
    1 SAM brigade (Improved Hawk)
  Hawaii
    1 infantry division (−1 brigade)
Europe
West Germany
    2 corps HQ
    2 armoured divisions

UNITED STATES OF AMERICA

2 mechanised divisions
1 armoured brigade
2 mechanised brigades
2 armoured cavalry regiments
West Berlin
  1 infantry brigade (+)
There are liaison and training missions together with HQ elements in the following countries:
Greece
Italy
Turkey

Equipment: The USA is the largest exporter of military equipment in the Western world. She is truly the arsenal of NATO and her enormous manufacturing capacity ensures that her allies will never go short of essential defence hardware. The only flaw in this imposing picture is the lack of a truly capable MBT. Successive attempts to produce a cooperative venture with other NATO countries have failed and the army is still fielding a tank that is basically a mid-1950s improved version of a Second World War medium. This will be corrected when the Abrams XM-1 is fully in service, but that will be many years yet. In all other equipment areas it is safe to say that US designs are ahead of their Soviet contemporaries, and sometimes very far ahead, though the gap is closing as budget restrictions have hampered R & D and closed government arsenals. Probably the most significant advances have been in missiles, particularly anti-armour missiles, and here the US Army is well placed.

AFVs	Tanks	M48A5	(USA)	1825
		M60	(USA)	1500
		M60A1	(USA)	5875
		M60A2	(USA)	540
		M60A3	(USA)	615
		M551	(USA)	1600
	APCs	M113	(USA)	}22 000
		M577	(USA)	
		M706 Commando	(USA)	
	SP guns	203 mm M110/110A1/2	(USA)	}4000
		155 mm M109/M109A1/2/3	(USA)	

UPPER VOLTA

Artillery	203 mm M115	(USA)	}	
	155 mm M114/M198	(USA)	} 2500	
	105 mm M101	(USA)	}	
	Honest John SSM	(USA)		
	Pershing SSM	(USA)		
	Lance SSM	(USA)		
	20 mm, 40 mm LAA	(USA)	600	
	Chaparral, Vulcan AA systems	(USA)		
	Redeye SAM	(USA)		
	Stinger SAM	(USA)	20 000	
	Nike Hercules SAM	(USA)		
	Improved Hawk SAM	(USA)		
Anti-tank	90 mm RCL, 106 mm RCL	(USA)	6000	
	Dragon ATGW	(USA)		
	TOW ATGW	(USA)		
Mortars	107 mm M30 (4.2 in)	(USA)	2000	
	81 mm M29/29A1	(USA)	3500	
Infantry	All weapons US designs, though Belgian MGs are being introduced			

Strength: 4000
Para-military forces, 1800 Gendarmerie
Military service: Two years conscription
Background: The country is very poor and deeply affected by the Sahel drought. The army is small and the main role is internal security with any question of frontier defence coming second. There have been border disputes with neighbours which were relatively low key. The army is almost entirely based on French methods and traditions and it is said to be rather better disciplined than many others of a similar size and background.

Structure
5 infantry battalions
1 reconnaissance squadron
1 'parachute' company
1 artillery battery

Equipment

AFVs

Armoured cars	AML-60/90	(France)
	M8	(USA)
Scout cars	Ferret	(UK)
Artillery	105 mm M101 howitzer	(USA)
Mortars	81 mm	(France)
Infantry	Mixture of French, West German and Swiss weapons	

URUGUAY

Strength: 20 000
Reserves, approximately 120 000. Para-military gendarmerie 2200
Military service: Voluntary
Background: The two most important roles of the army are internal security and defence of the national frontiers. For the last 10 years internal security has dominated the military activities as the Tupamaros gangs kidnapped and raided, but strong action by both the army and the police has now overcome them. The army is now closely involved in politics, but it is hoped to end this soon. The voluntary recruits are normally trained in their units, with specialist training undertaken in central schools. The Reserve receives no refresher training so its value may be less than its numbers suggest, but there is little chance of it being needed.
Structure: There are four military regions, with an administrative HQ in each. Operationally the highest formation is the unit, and the greatest concentration of units is in the two regions around the capital city, Montevideo.

4 regional HQ
3 armoured regiments
6 cavalry regiments
13 infantry battalions
4 artillery battalions (battery strength only)
1 AA battalion
5 engineer battalions

Equipment: There is sufficient industry to produce small arms ammunition and some spares for service equipment. Most of the weapons and equipment are elderly and US in origin.

AFVs Tanks	M24	(USA)	17
	M3A1 light	(USA)	18
Scout cars	M3A1	(USA)	10
APCs	M113	(USA)	15
Artillery	105 mm M101 howitzer	(USA)	25
	75 mm M116 pack	(USA)	
Infantry	US weapons		

VENEZUELA

Strength: 28 000
Reserves, no formed reserves. National Guard 10 000
Military service: Two years selective conscription
Background: The army has always acted as the prop and support of the government of the day and has been a force in the background for the implementing of policy. To a great extent this is now changing, but it is taking time. A guerrilla threat in the Andean region has necessitated the raising of new ranger battalions to counter it and as a result the size of the army has increased. Recruits are given their training in units and on leaving the army they may join the National Guard. The latter has a high standing in the country and is largely responsible for internal security. Operationally, the army could put up a limited defence against an invasion, but would be unable to mount more than a very small offensive force.
Structure: In general the army has its larger bases near to the capital and in the Andean region. The usual operational grouping is in individual units and there is no attempt to form larger formations.
 3 armoured battalions
 2 mechanised infantry battalions
11 infantry battalions
13 ranger (light infantry) battalions
 1 horsed cavalry regiment
 7 artillery groups
 5 engineer battalions
   AA groups

Equipment: There is no arms industry at all and all equipment has been imported from USA. In recent years, however purchases have been made from France and a few other European countries.

AFVs	Tanks	AMX-30	(France)	142
		AMX-13 light	(France)	40
	Armoured cars	M8	(USA)	12
	APCs	AMX-VC1	(France)	
		UR-416	(West Germany)	20
	SP guns	155 mm Mk F3	(France)	20
		76 mm M18	(USA)	35
Artillery		105 mm M101	(USA)	135
		105 mm Model 56 pack	(Italy)	
		75 mm M116 pack	(USA)	
		40 mm Bofors LAA	(USA/Sweden)	
Anti-tank		106 mm M40A1 RCL	(USA)	
		SS11 ATGW	(France)	
Mortars		120 mm	(France)	
		81 mm	(France)	
Infantry		Most weapons originate from Belgium but there are some Italian and West German SMGs		

VIET-NAM

Strength: 1 000 000
Reserves, Militia and various armed para-military forces, approximately 2 000 000
Military service: Two years
Background: The army is the third largest in Asia, after the Chinese and the Indian and it is also one of the best equipped and far and away the most experienced. Quite how much longer the country can continue to support the enormous numbers of soldiers is not at all clear, but it may be that before long some are returned to the labour pool. Meanwhile, the army continues to occupy Kampuchea and to continue with its operations in Laos. Information on such details as training is hard to come by, but it is known that the army follows the usual communist system and it must be assumed that its soldiers are supervised and trained more or less continually during their two years of service. After that they return to their homes and probably form part of the enormous People's Militia which would defend the homeland in time of war.
Structure: Apparently the main formation is the division, as in other communist armies, and it is not likely that there is any need for a higher formation. Many of the divisional and regimental numberings go back to the Vietcong war, and perhaps even further, and it must be assumed now that the large South Vietnamese Army (ARVN) has been assimilated together with its equipment.

1 armoured division
28 infantry divisions
2 artillery divisions
1 AA division
1 engineer division
5 independent armoured regiments
15 independent motorised infantry regiments
35 independent artillery regiments
50 independent AA artillery regiments
25 SAM regiments
15 independent engineer regiments

Deployment
Laos 40 000
Kampuchea 100 000+

Equipment: For years there has been a fragmented arms industry in North Viet-Nam which has reached a fair standard of efficiency. It largely produces ammunition though there is also the capacity to make some small automatic weapons. However, all bulk supplies have to be imported from China or the USSR. The inherited US equipment may be a mixed blessing since there are neither spares nor ammunition for them.

AFVs Tanks	T-34/54/55/62	(USSR)	} 1000
	Type 59/60/62/63	(PRC)	
	PT-76 light	(USSR)	} 450
	Type 60 light	(PRC)	
	M47/48	(USA)	400
	M41 light	(USA)	150
Armoured cars	M8	(USA)	
	M20	(USA)	
	BRDM	(USSR)	
APCs	BTR-40/50/60/152	(USSR)	} 1000
	Type 56/63	(PRC)	
	M113	(USA)	} 800
	V-150 Commando	(USA)	
SP guns	203 mm M110	(USA)	
	175 mm M107	(USA)	} 200
	155 mm M109	(USA)	
	105 mm M108	(USA)	
	100 mm SU-100	(USSR)	} 90
	76 mm SU-76	(USSR)	
Artillery	155 mm M114	(USA)	} 800
	105 mm M101	(USA)	
	152 mm M1937/D-1	(USSR)	100
	130 mm M46	(USSR)	200
	122 mm D-30/D-74/ M1931/M1938	(USSR)	800

	100 mm M1955/1944	(USSR)	
	85 mm D-44	(USSR)	} 300
	76 mm M1942	(USSR)	
	75 mm M116 pack	(USA)	
	140 mm BM-41 RL	(USSR)	
	122 mm BM-21 RL	(USSR)	
	107 mm Type 63 RL	(PRC)	
	85 mm, 100 mm AA	(USSR)	
	23 mm, 37 mm, 57 mm LAA	(USSR)	
	ZSU-23-4, ZSU-57-2 SP LAA	(USSR)	} 8000
	SA-2/3/6/9 SAM	(USSR)	
Anti-tank	107 mm B-11 RCL	(USSR)	
	106 mm M40A1 RCL	(USA)	
	82 mm B-10 RCL	(USSR)	
	75 mm Type 52/56 RCL	(PRC)	
	Sagger ATGW	(USSR)	
Mortars	160 mm M60	(USSR)	
	120 mm M43	(USSR)	
	107 mm (4.2 in) M30	(USA)	
	82 mm M37	(USSR)	
Infantry	Largely equipped with Soviet designs, but some US equipment must be presumed to be used also		

YEMEN ARAB REPUBLIC (NORTH)

Strength: 35 000 approximately
Reserves, approximately 20 000 para-military tribesmen
Military service: Three years
Background: The main role of the army is to maintain internal security and to support the central government against the often insurgent tribes. This has led it into conflict with South Yemen which gives aid to the tribes and there have been more or less serious clashes between the two countries, with North Yemen by no means getting the best of the argument. A difficulty is that after some years of Soviet military aid and training missions the army is now turning more and more to Western equipment and assistance, all this sponsored by Saudi Arabia who wishes to have a friendly neighbour untainted by communism. The army is finding the transition a slow process which reduces efficiency. It can best be described as a defensive force with little or no offensive capability.
Structure: The organisation is still Soviet and so are the tactical principles. The main formation is the brigade and these are now up to strength.
2 infantry divisions
2 armoured brigades
1 parachute brigade
2 commando brigades
5 artillery battalions
2 AA battalions

Equipment: There is no arms industry and all equipment is imported. The recent shipments of US weapons will be causing some maintenance troubles since the army is traditionally armed with Soviet equipment.

AFVs Tanks	M60	(USA)	32
	T-34/54	(USSR)	200
Armoured cars	Ferret	(UK)	} 50
	Saladin	(UK)	
APCs	M113	(USA)	50
	BTR-40/152	(USSR)	} 350
	Walid	(Egypt)	
SP guns	100 mm SU-100	(USSR)	50
Artillery	122 mm M1931	(USSR)	} 50
	76 mm M1942	(USSR)	
	20 mm, 37 mm,		
	57 mm LAA	(USA/USSR)	
	20 mm M163		
	SP LAA	(USA)	
Anti-tank	75 mm M20 RCL	(USA)	
	Vigilant ATGW	(UK)	
Mortars	120 mm M43	(USSR)	
Infantry	Mixture of British, Italian and Soviet weapons, the latter predominating		

Strength: 19 000

Reserves, 15 000 para-military militia

Military service: Two years

Background: South Yemen is surrounded by countries which are more or less hostile to the regime and the role of the army is to defend the national territory. It also carries out raids and incursions over the frontiers, something that does little for peace in the area. Training is supervised by both Soviet and Cuban advisers and is all along normal Soviet lines. The ability of the army to fight a prolonged war is doubtful, but it could certainly conduct a defensive fight with some skill.

Structure: Organisation is the normal one on Soviet lines and there is no detailed information on deployment within the country, however it is known that there are always some units along the northern and Omani borders.

10 infantry brigades (3 battalions in each)

2 armoured battalions

5 artillery battalions

1 signals unit

1 training battalion

Equipment: Most of the equipment is Soviet in origin, however there is a surprising amount of elderly British equipment from the time before 1970 when a lot was handed over. The state of maintenance is not known.

AFVs	Tanks	T-34/54	(USSR)	250
	Armoured cars	Saladin	(UK)	10
		Ferret	(UK)	10
APCs		BTR-40/152	(USSR)	
Artillery		130 mm M46	(USSR)	
		122 mm M1938	(USSR)	
		105 mm Model 56 pack	(Italy/UK)	
		25 pdr	(UK)	
		122 mm BM-21 RL	(USSR)	
		85 mm, 100 mm AA	(USSR)	
		23 mm, 37 mm, 57 mm LAA	(USSR)	
		SA-6/9 SAM		
Mortars		120 mm M43	(USSR)	
Infantry		Mixture of British and Soviet with the latter more usually found		

YUGOSLAVIA

Strength: 190 000 (130 000 conscripts)
Reserves, 500 000. 1 000 000+ TA and para-military forces
Military service: 15 months
Background: Yugoslavia is committed to a policy of 'Total Defence' which effectively means that all citizens are expected to take part in armed resistance against an invader. It is a bold concept, but it is expensive and it takes much effort to implement. The country belongs to no military alliances and remains staunchly neutral. Whether this deterrent attitude is really viable can be debated, but it has worked for 30 years so far. All training is aimed at defence and the army could not be expected to mount any practical offensive operations beyond its own borders. Motivation is good and apparently morale remains high. From time to time there are mobilisation and formation exercises to test the general system and to practise the reserve call-up arrangements.
Structure: The regular army is organised with proper support services and arms. Divisions are made up from three brigades but brigades may have more than three battalions. In the case of the tank brigade it is possible to have three tank battalions and two or three infantry battalions, making it a large formation nearer in strength to a small division. The Reserve Army tends to be more of a static organisation based regionally and relying on local reinforcements. There is, however, a manoeuvre element in it which would carry out mobile operations.

9 infantry divisions
11 independent infantry brigades
7 independent tank brigades
1 mountain brigade
1 airborne battalion
9 artillery regiments
5 anti-tank regiments
15 AA regiments

Equipment: The army uses a wide range of equipment emanating from several sources and of widely differing ages. There are still some Second World War designs in use, but also some of the latest models. There is a flourishing arms industry with a steady export trade, particularly in ammunition.

AFVs	Tanks			
		M4 Sherman	(USA)	650
		T-34/54/55	(USSR)	1500
		M47	(USA)	
		PT-76 light	(USSR)	
	Armoured cars	M3	(USA)	
		M8	(USA)	
		BRDM-2	(USSR)	
	APCs	M980	(Yugoslavia)	
		BTR-50/60/152	(USSR)	
		M-60	(Yugoslavia)	
	SP guns	105 mm M7	(USA)	
		100 mm SU-100	(USSR)	
		90 mm M36	(USA)	

Artillery		
	76 mm M18	(USA)
	155 mm M59/65	(Yugoslavia)
	155 mm M114	(USA)
	152 mm M1937	(USSR)
	130 mm M46	(USSR)
	122 mm D-30/ M1931/38	(USSR)
	105 mm M101/ 56/18/18-40	(USA)
	100 mm M1942/ 55	(USSR)
	76 mm M-48 mountain	(Yugoslavia)
	128 mm M-63 YMRL-32 RL	(Yugoslavia)
	Frog SSM	(USSR)
	90 mm M17 AA	(USA)
	85 mm KS-12 AA	(USSR)
	30 mm, 37 mm, 40 mm 57 mm LAA	(Yugoslavia & USSR)
	20 mm M-30/ 38 LAA	(Yugoslavia)
	SA-6/9 SAM	(USSR)

Anti-tank		
	75 mm, 82 mm, 107 mm RCL	(USSR/ Yugoslavia)
	Snapper, Sagger ATGW	(USSR)

Mortars Infantry		
	120 mm UBM 52	(Yugoslavia)

Largely equipped with Yugoslav variants of Soviet designs. The standard MG is a German design made in Yugoslavia

Yugoslav gunners with ex-British 3.7-in gun. (I. V. Hogg)

ZAÏRE

Strength: 18 500
Reserves, 30 000+ para-military forces
Military service: Voluntary
Background: The army has the usual two roles of defending the country and maintaining internal security. It has had plenty of practice at both and has shown itself to be less than competent in either field. The army appears to be used for whatever task the President deems to be the priority of the day. Thus it has been given the twin aim of rural development and political education, though there was such discontent that these were cancelled. The most recent occasion when the army failed to put down a small incursion resulted in the well-known French/Moroccan intervention at Kolwezi. From this it can be gathered that the standards of training are poor and motivation is not high.
Structure: Units are grouped into regional districts known as brigade groups but the actual operational formation is the battalion/regiment.
 3 infantry brigade HQs
 3 armoured regiments
 2 mechanised battalions
10 infantry battalions
 2 parachute battalions (below strength, under-trained)
 1 commando battalion

Equipment: All equipment is imported and it has come from many different sources. The state of maintenance is unlikely to be high.

AFVs Tanks	Type 62 light	(PRC)	38
Armoured cars	AML-60	(France)	95
	AML-90	(France)	40
APCs	M3	(USA)	60
	M113	(USA)	9
Artillery	130 mm M46	(USSR)	
	122 mm M1938	(USSR)	
	75 mm M116 pack	(USA)	
	40 mm Bofors L60 LAA	(Sweden)	
	37 mm M1939 LAA	(USSR)	
Anti-tank	75 mm M20 RCL	(USA)	
Mortars	107 mm (4.2 in) M30	(USA)	
Infantry	Mixture of US and Belgian weapons		

ZAMBIA

Strength: 12 800
Reserves, approximately 2000 para-military forces
Military service: Voluntary
Background: The main troubles in Zambia are national cohesion and frontier incursions. The latter will reduce now that Zimbabwe is peaceful, but it has been a difficult 10 years for Zambia and the army has suffered. Training has been carried out by a number of different national teams, including Cuban (not confirmed). There is not sufficient money to maintain the army properly and this is reflected in a variable state of morale and efficiency.
Structure: The general structure is still the old British one left when independence was gained in 1964. There is no attempt to use units at more than individual level and they are generally thought to be stationed either in the capital or on the frontiers.

1 armoured car regiment
4 infantry battalions
1 artillery battalion
1 AA regiment
1 engineer squadron
1 signals squadron

Equipment: There is no arms industry and all equipment is imported.

AFVs Tanks	T-54	(USSR)	30
Scout cars	Ferret	(UK)	28
Artillery	105 mm Model 56 pack	(Italy)	8
	20 mm LAA		24
Infantry	Wide mixture of weapons		

ZIMBABWE

Strength: Approximately 15 000
Reserves, not known
Military service: Voluntary
Background: The army is being re-formed after the disastrous civil war and it will be some time before it settles into a recognisable pattern. The main task at present is to integrate white with the two rival black groups. The resulting army will no doubt inherit some of the characteristics of its predecessor and will be a lightly-armed high-mobility force with the accent on infantry. Its employment is more problematical, but internal security is likely to be the main task for many years to come.
Structure: It is early to be defining the structure, but it is likely to be a series of independent units intended to fight on their own rather than in formations. The largest formation will probably be the brigade.

1 armoured car regiment
4 or 5 infantry battalions
  independent infantry companies
  engineer and signals units
1 or 2 artillery regiments

Equipment: There is a small industry making spares and a limited number of light small arms, as well as the conversion of trucks into armoured vehicles. However, Zimbabwe has for a long time depended on elderly British equipment which has been kept working by skilful mechanics.

AFVs

Armoured cars	AML-90	(France)	60
	Eland	(Zimbabwe)	
Scout cars	Ferret	(UK)	
APCs	UR-416	(West Germany)	
Artillery	5.5 in medium gun	(UK)	
	105 mm Model 56 pack	(Italy)	
	25 pdr	(UK)	
Infantry	Belgian and West German rifles. Many British MGs and mortars		